B. Kaufmann/MICHELIN — The Patio de los Leones, one of the marvels of the Alhambra — 1

CONTENTS

Introduction

Background

Highlights

Exploring the city

2

Monuments and sights of interest

Excursions

Directory

Index

"**G**ive him alms, woman, for there is no greater pain in life than being blind in Granada." This popular saying, inscribed on a wall in the Alhambra, evokes the beauty of this city, its delightful **setting***** and its monuments, the jewel of which is the Alhambra itself, one of the most magnificent artistic creations ever to have been built by man.

Granada is situated in a wide fertile plain dissected by the River Genil and River Darro. The city spreads majestically upwards on the evocatively named hills of the Albaicín, Sacromonte and Alhambra – Granada's Moorish quarter – which overlook the modern, Christian city sitting compactly at their feet. This magnificent city, with its sumptuous monuments, is protected by the lofty, snow-capped outline of the Sierra Nevada.

Yet Granada is more than just a single monument. It is a city of history indelibly marked by its splendid Moorish and Christian past. By taking the time to wander through the old narrow streets, idle away a hot summer's afternoon in one of the city's shady squares, and explore its less-vaunted treasures, visitors will soon discover that Granada is as unforgettable as it is beautiful.

Imagen © TURISMO ANDALUZ S.A.

4

Introduction

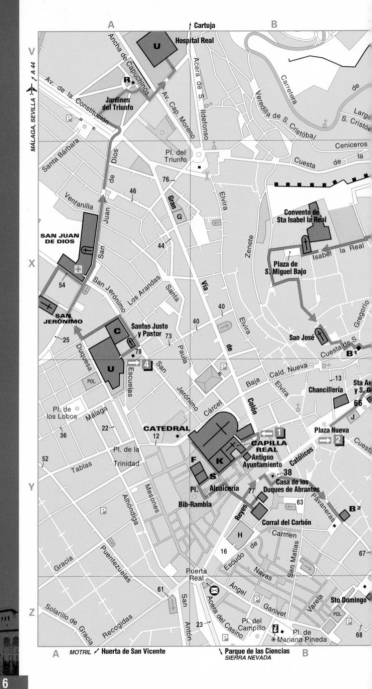

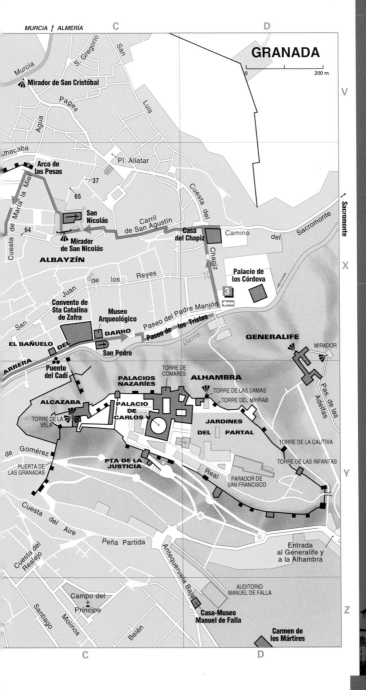

━━ See "Exploring the city"

Population: 241 471. Michelin map 578 U 19. Michelin Granada city plan 83.

Granada is situated at the confluence of the River Genil and River Darro, in a privileged location at the centre of the province of the same name, a little over 30km/18mi from the Sierra Nevada ski resort and just 70km/44mi from the Mediterranean. The city stands at the crossroads of the A 44-E 902 and A 92 motorways, with excellent road links to Jaén (94km/59mi N), Málaga (124km/77mi SW), Almería (171km/107mi SE) and Sevilla (250km/156mi W).

Granada is a delightful city to explore on foot, in particular the historical centre and Albaicín, with its narrow streets and alleyways.

🚹 *Plaza de Mariana Pineda, 10,* ☎ *958 24 71 28.*

Location

12

B. Kaufmann/MICHELIN

Background

Historical outline

BACKGROUND

Granada's origins are somewhat vague, although it is known that Iberian settlements existed here, and that the Romans founded a colony known as Illiberis on the Albaicín hill. Despite these periods of colonisation, the city was of little importance until the arrival of the Moors in the early 8C.

Moorish Granada

In 713, Tarik's troops conquered the city, which at the time extended across the Alhambra and Albaicín hills. During the Cordoban Caliphate, the city came under the rule of its northern neighbour, although when the latter broke up, in 1013, it became the capital of an independent kingdom (taifa), governed by the **Zirite dynasty**. The Zirites strengthened the city's defences and built the El Bañuelo baths and a bridge, the Puente de Cadí.

In 1090, Granada fell into the hands of the **Almoravids**, who were subsequently overthrown by the **Almohads** in the middle of the 12C. Despite

frequent internecine conflicts, the city underwent considerable development during this 150-year period, including the establishment of drainage and sewerage systems, and the further strengthening of its fortifications.

Nasrid kingdom – The rise to power of the Nasrid dynasty in 1238 heralded the beginning of the city's Golden Age. The agreement signed between Fernando III and Mohammed ibn Nasar, the dynasty's founder, through which the Moorish leader acknowledged his position as the king's vassal, resulted in a period of stability and calm.

In addition to Granada, the kingdom encompassed the provinces of Almería and Málaga, and part of the provinces of Cádiz, Sevilla, Córdoba and Jaén. During this period, its capital, Granada, prospered and entered a phase of great embellishment. The city extended its boundaries to its lower sections, and construction of the Alhambra commenced. Yusuf I (1333-53) and Mohammed V (1353-91), under whose rule the Alhambra's Nasrid palaces were built, transformed Granada into one of the leading cities of the period.

The 15C was marked by infighting which facilitated the Christians' task of gradually reducing the size of the Nasrid kingdom. Following a long

THE TEARS OF BOABDIL

Having handed over the keys to Granada, Boabdil, the last Nasrid king, began his journey into exile. At the place that has gone down in history with the name of The Moor's Sigh (*Suspiro del Moro*), he stopped to cast a final glance at his beloved city, but was unable to hold back his tears. His mother is said to have rounded on him: "You weep like a woman for what you could not hold as a man."

siege, the Catholic Monarchs took the city on 2 January 1492, closing a chapter of Moorish domination on the Iberian Peninsula lasting eight centuries.

Christian Granada

Following the reconquest of Granada, the city's *morisco* population established their community on the Albaicín. However, by the end of the 15C the first in a series of conflicts had broken out following the decision to force Muslims to be baptised. As the years passed, the situation worsened, reaching a climax in 1568 when the leader of the revolt, Abén Humeya, fled to the Alpujarras mountains, where he was defeated by Don Juan of Austria, on the orders of Felipe II. Following this bloody episode, all *moriscos* were expelled from Granada.

During the 16C and 17C, the city experienced significant development with the razing of the maze-like network of Moorish streets to create wider streets and spacious squares, and the construction of important buildings such as the cathedral, Royal Chapel, Charles V's palace, the Exchange, Royal Hospital, chancery and Carthusian monastery.

In the 18C, and particularly the 19C, Granada assumed great popularity with numerous visitors who were bewitched by its charms. Romanticism was to forge a new image for a city which was long used to having its praises sung. Its beauty, tinged with an aura of mysticism and exoticism, became a literary theme for renowned writers such as Victor Hugo, Alexandre Dumas and Washington Irving, who penned his famous *Tales of the Alhambra*. However, during the 19C Granada was to receive other, less welcome visitors in the shape of French troops who destroyed parts of the city during their period of occupation. Thankfully, their attempts to destroy the Alhambra resulted in no more than the loss of some of its towers and various sections of its defensive walls.

Granada today

Nowadays, the city is the capital of a province whose main income derives from agriculture, cattle breeding and tourism. It is a lively city all year round, an atmosphere generated by the students from its respected university, and the thousands of annual visitors. The local *granadinos* believe that their city has the perfect location: on the doorstep of the Sierra Nevada with its sun-blessed ski slopes, and just an hour's drive from the Mediterranean, offering the perfect escape from the summer heat.

Carlos V's palace

Hispano-Moorish art (8c-15c)

The Moorish invasion, which initially appeared as a tragic event in the history of the Iberian Peninsula, was in fact the catalyst for several centuries of great splendour, resulting in a fusion of creativity and aesthetic ideas that saw the construction of magnificent palaces, mosques and fortresses unique in Europe at the time.

During the eight centuries of Muslim presence in Spain from the 8C-15C, the art of al-Andalus always retained a series of basic characteristics which clearly set it part from any other artistic trend during this period.

Arches

During the early days of Moorish rule, the **horseshoe arch**, with its Visigothic and Oriental influence and alternating red (brick) and white (plaster with lime) voussoirs, was the main feature used in Moorish buildings. The arches had a dual purpose: as an element of support and as a decorative feature, for example to act as a border for a blind arch. The development of intercrossing arches gave rise to the pointed horseshoe-shaped arch, which was extensively used from the 12C onwards.

As time passed, the **foliated arch**, which was already in evi-

The star-shaped cupola of the Sala de los Abencerrajes

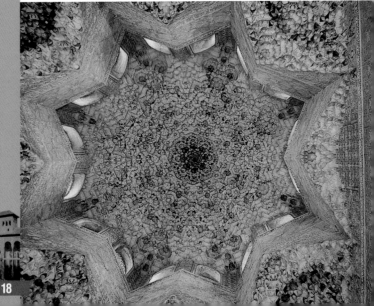

dence in the Mezquita in Córdoba, evolved into the highly complex **multifoil arch**.

The **alfiz**, the rectangular moulding surrounding the arch, was another of the recurrent themes of Moorish art, and was to have a major influence on Mudéjar art in subsequent centuries.

Vaults, armatures and artesonado work

Hispano-Moorish vaults took their influence from Oriental Islamic art. Unlike those used in Christian art (arris and fan vaults), their ribs do not cross in the centre of the vault. Perhaps one of the best examples of this can be seen in the enclosure of the mihrab in Córdoba's Mezquita.

Yet, despite the uniqueness of Andalusian vaults, it is undoubtedly the widely used wooden armature which can be considered as the architectural feature which best displays the Moor's technical and aesthetic expertise. Wooden coverings evolved from simple paired and knuckle armatures to the most sophisticated of artesonado work decorated with stars to form attractive lacería ornamentation.

Decoration: materials and motifs

Hidden behind the austerity of their external walls, the interiors of Andalusian palaces were often of extraordinary splendour, although the rendering used within them often completely masked the poor quality of the construction materials.

The refined aesthetic sense of the Hispano-Moors managed to successfully combine techniques as disparate as **azulejos** and **alicatados** (decorative sections of tiling), panels of stone or sculpted plasterwork, mosaics with Oriental influence, wood worked to form latticework, and exquisite *artesonado*, to create surprisingly sumptuous effects.

The decorative motifs used can be classified into three main groups:

– **geometric designs**, mainly used in the decoration of glazed ceramic friezes and in the ornamentation of wood (doors, latticework and artesonados), in which the lines are broken up by polygons and stars;

– **plant motifs**, which were known as **atauriques**, used to decorate sculpted stone or plaster wall panels. With the passing of time, these motifs (palm leaves, grapevines) were styled to create extremely complex designs. One of the most common techniques used was the stylisation of the tree of life – vegetal decoration arranged around a vertical axis. Mocárabes, decorative motifs resembling stalactites, were used to decorate arches and cupolas;

– **epigraphs** fulfilled the same informative function as images used by other architectural styles, with **Kufic script**, characterised by its large, angled lettering, and **Nesjí script**, with its more free-flowing characters, the most widely used. Three types of inscriptions were used in

Nasrid buildings in Granada: those providing information on the building's origins; religious inscriptions, citing verses from the Koran; and literary and poetic prose.

Applied arts

Andalusian decorative art produced a variety of elaborate objects which can be separated into two distinct groups, namely household and luxury items, the latter created to satisfy the demand of a more refined ruling class who afforded greater importance to interior decoration and who took great pleasure in bestowing unique and sumptuous gifts on foreign visitors.

J. Bouraly/MICHELIN

In terms of **ceramics**, the following stand out: the earthenware known as **green and manganese**, the so-called **cuerda seca** ceramics (azulejos) used as wall decoration, and the gilded work known as **reflejo metálico** (lustre work). The latter, production of which began in Córdoba in the 9C, attained its full glory during the Nasrid period in the production centres in and around Málaga.

In addition to Córdoba, where Abd ar-Rahman II founded the Casa del Tiraz or Royal Silk Factory, during the 14C and 15C, the workshops of Granada also produced impressive silk fabrics entwined with gold thread. In

Detail, the magnificent decoration of the Nasrides

general, intense colours predominated in these fabrics, which were decorated with inscriptions and architectural motifs.

Nasrid **gold and silversmiths** showed a special predilection for ceremonial swords, the hilts and guards of which were decorated with extraordinary combinations of marble, filigree and polychrome enamel.

To complete the full picture of Hispano-Moorish artistry, mention should also be made of the highly delicate **marble carvings**, which were popular decorative features used by the Caliphate, taraceas (**marble-inlaid** wood and wood of varying colours) used to decorate Nasrid furniture, and leatherwork (**cordovans** made from goatskin and embossed **guadamecies** made from sheepskin).

Many of these items remained popular over the centuries due to their continued use by the Christians, who praised their quality and value. As an example to illustrate this, the sculpted marble boxes and chests used by Muslim women to keep their jewels and perfume were subsequently used to preserve the relics of saints.

Nasrid period (13C-15C)

In the eyes of many specialists, this era represents the greatest period in Andalusian art. For many years, these same experts highlighted the poverty of the materials used in Nasrid art, and their contrast with their abundance of decoration. Nowadays it is known that the function of the building determined the choice of materials used in its construction. Consequently, in baths, as well as fortresses such as the Alcazaba in Granada, ashlar ctone, bricks and mortar (consisting of its characteristic red colour) were used, while palaces such as the Alhambra used **marble** on the floors and for its columns, **glazed ceramics** (azulejos) in areas exposed to friction, **elaborate plaster and stucco decoration**, wooden vaults and artesonados and **mocárabe vaults**.

Capitals were generally of two types: the first had a cylindrical base decorated with plain leaves which supported a parallelepiped adorned with additional foliage; the second type were mocárabe in style and derived from Oriental art.

Although less spectacular nowadays due to the weathering effects of time, **colour** was the other main feature of Nasrid buildings, the interiors of which, in their prime, must have looked like an Impressionist painting. In addition to the friezes of azulejos, the plaster and wood used to cover walls were painted in red, blue, green and gold tones, at a time when different coloured marble was also used for capitals and columns. Given that the present-day appearance of the Alhambra continues to impress and amaze millions of visitors, we can only imagine how impressive it must have looked during its period of ultimate splendour.

J. Bouraly/MICHELIN

Detail, The Patio de los Leones, the Alhambra Palace

The Moorish garden: a paradise on Earth

The Moors were truly gifted gardeners. A Moorish garden is always an evocation of paradise; it is a feast for the senses and a harmonious whole which avoids grandiloquence. Nothing has been left to chance: the colour of the plants and flowers, their scent, and the omnipresence of water combine to create a serene ambience full of intimate charm.

The Generalife is *the* Moorish garden par excellence, despite the alterations it has undergone over the centuries. As a result of its extraordinary position it is a magnificent balcony, but above all it has been able to preserve an intimate, sensual character which was such a feature of Muslim gardens.

The Generalife has been laid out on several levels to ensure that the trees in one garden do not interfere with the views from another. In fact, the Generalife is a series of landscaped areas and enclosures each with its own individuality yet part of an overall design. The garden's architectural features and vegetation, reflected in the water channels, blend together to create a perfect whole.

Throughout the kingdom of al-Andalus, that scarce commodity – water – played a fundamental role in architecture. Water had a triple function: practical, religious and aesthetic. Practical, because of its necessity for life (the irrigation of fields and the supply of bath water); religious, because the Koran states that a series of ablutions must be carried out prior to prayer; and aesthetic, because water stored in pools and basins reflected the elegant decoration of the walls and ceilings, while water running through channels, fountains and gutters produced a relaxing murmuring and provided welcome cool. Water also enabled gardens to be created that were so well integrated into the surrounding architecture that it is difficult to know where nature ends and where the works created by man begin.

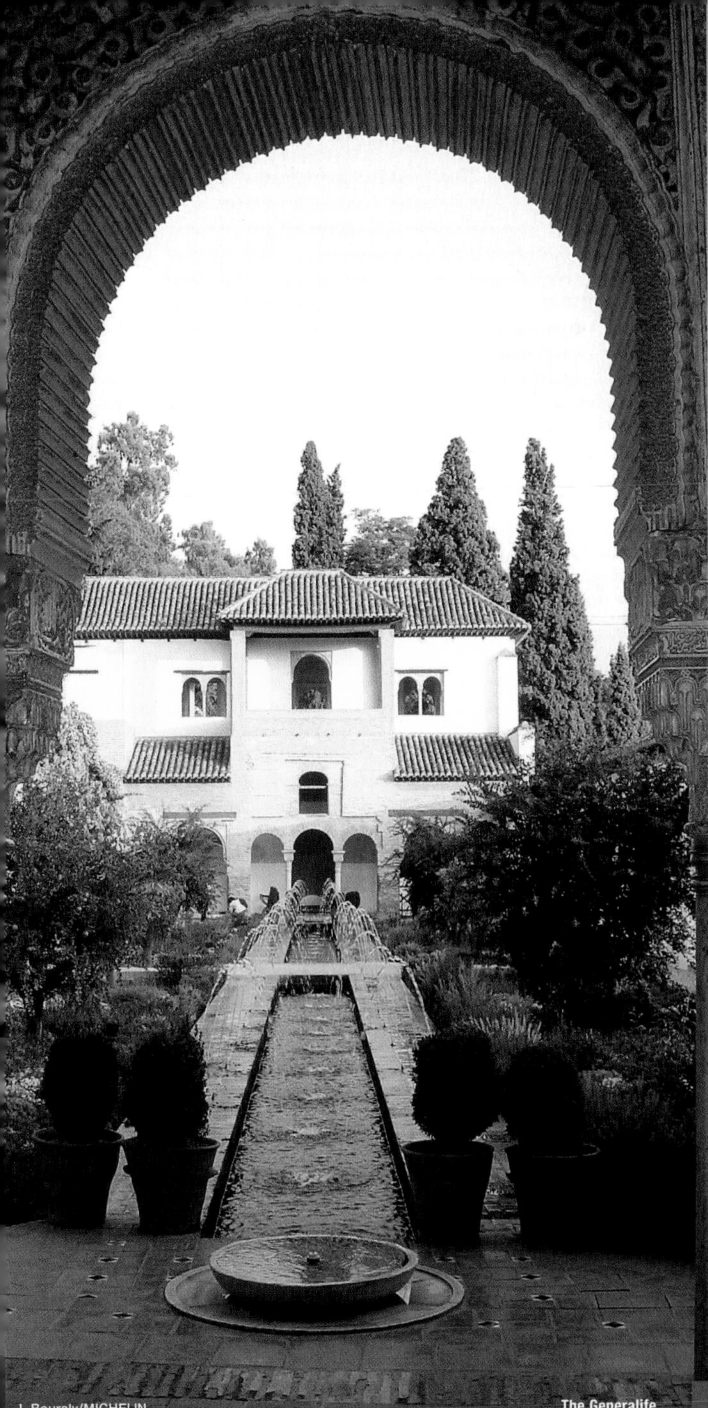

J. Bouraly/MICHELIN

The Generalife

Fiestas and festivals

Toma de Granada

The first important festival in the Andalusian calendar takes place on 2 January to commemorate a key historical event in Spanish history: Boabdil's surrender to the massed Christian armies and the subsequent capture (toma) of Granada by the Catholic Monarchs. The procession, headed by the standard of Fernando and Isabel, climbs up to the Torre de la Vela in the Alhambra, where the tower's bell is then rung. According to tradition, those young women who take part in the fiesta will be married by the end of the year.

San Cecilio

The saint's day of St Cecilio (1 February), the city's patron, is celebrated by a religious pilgrimage (romería) to the Sacramonte district, where jugs of wine and broad beans (habas) are distributed to the city's inhabitants next to the local abbey. This fiesta is also a time for the dancing and singing of the traditional sevillanas.

Semana Santa

In contrast to other Andalusian cities, Granada's Holy Week is typified by restraint and silence. From Palm Sunday to Easter Sunday, myriad processions file along the steep, cobbled Official Route (Carrera Oficial), which terminates at the cathedral. Valuable Baroque statues by masters such as Diego de Siloé, Pedro de Mena, Giacomo Fiorentino and their contemporaries are carried aloft by the traditional costaleros, who are forced to their knees in order to squeeze their impressive floats (pasos) through the cathedral's narrow ogival doorway.

Las Cruces de Mayo

The Festival of the May Crosses on 3 May sees the city's streets and patios adorned with flower-decked crosses.

Corpus Christi

Granada's main week of festivities, when the city hosts its annual fair (feria), numerous bullfights and other events, coincides with the solemn Corpus Christi procession, when the streets are carpeted in flowers and aromatic herbs.

Festivals

The city hosts a range of important cultural events throughout the year. These include the International Theatre Festival (in May, at the Teatro Manuel de Falla), the International Music and Dance Festival (in June and July, in the Alhambra; www.granadafestival.org), and the International Jazz Festival (October and November).

Imagen © TURISMO ANDALUZ S.A.

Cruz de Mayo

Highlights

Alhambra and Generalife ★★★

allow half a day

Access on foot to the Alhambra Palace and Generalife from the city centre is along cuesta de Gomérez, from plaza Nueva. Enter the outer perimeter of the palace through the Puerta de Granadas (Pomegranate Gate), built by Machuca during the reign of Emperor Charles V, to reach the **shrubbery***. For visitors arriving by car or bus, the main approach up to the Alhambra branches off the road heading towards the Sierra Nevada and is clearly signposted.

VISIT

☎ *902 441 221. Because of the Alhambra's huge popularity, visitors are advised to purchase entrance tickets in advance either from branches of the BBV bank anywhere in Spain or on the Alhambra website: www.alhambratickets.com. The same ticket covers all parts of the Alhambra and Generalife gardens and specifies the time for entry to the Nasrid palace.*

ALHAMBRA ★★★

The beautiful Calat Alhambra (Red Castle) must be one of the most remarkable fortresses ever built and the finest Moorish palace still standing anywhere in the world. It sits at the top of a wooded hill – the highest in the city – which in medieval times was known as La Sabika. "La Sabika is the crown on Granada's head... and the Alhambra (may God protect her) is the ruby on the crown" wrote the poet Ibn Zamrak (1333-93).

Visitors to the Alhambra are spellbound by its refinement and the splendour of its architecture which incorporates delightful gardens and running water into the overall plan, thus perpetuating the tradition of a Koranic Eden like no other building on Earth. However, its beauty is also full of contradictions, in that the sumptuous appearance of the individual architectural components contrasts with the poverty of the materials used to create them. It is also surprising that a political power in decline should build such a masterpiece and that the Alhambra would be so respected by those rulers who took its place in the years to come. Yet, despite its impressive dimensions, the

KEY DATES

The most accepted chronology for the construction of the Alhambra and Generalife is as follows:
– late 12C: external walls;
– 14C: the Generalife, then the Nasrid palaces, built during the reigns of Yusuf I (1333-54) and Mohammed V (1354-59 and 1362-91).

Patio de los Arrayanes

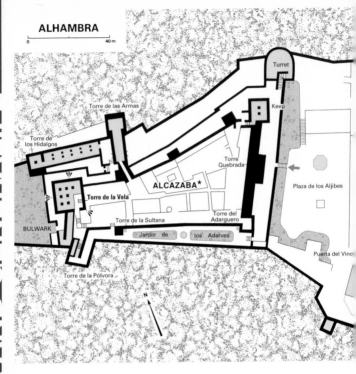

ALHAMBRA

0   40 m

Turret

Torre de las Armas

Keep

Torre de los Hidalgos

Torre Quebrada

ALCAZABA★

Plaza de los Aljibes

Torre de la Vela

Torre del Adarguero

BULWARK

Torre de la Sultana

Jardín de los Adarves

Puerta del Vino

Torre de la Pólvora

N

Alhambra is a palace that has been built on a scale that can be appreciated by modern-day visitors.

Nasrid palaces★★★
(Palacios Nazaríes)

These palaces are the central nucleus of the whole fortress. Nothing on their exterior presages their internal richness or the variety and decorative originality of their *mocárabe* vaults, domes, friezes and stuccowork which, combined with the effects of water and light – both of which are used as architectural features – create a jewel of incalculable value.

The buildings are around three courtyards: the Patio del Cuarto Dorado (Courtyard of the Golden Room), the Patio de los Arrayanes (Myrtle Courtyard) and the Patio de los Leones (Lion Courtyard). As a result of the palace's layout, in which the individual rooms are interconnected by small passageways, the visual impact as one passes from one architectural masterpiece to the next is all the more striking.

The Mexuar – The tour begins in the rectangular **Mexuar**. The four columns at the front support a stucco-adorned entablature. An attractive frieze of *azulejos* and

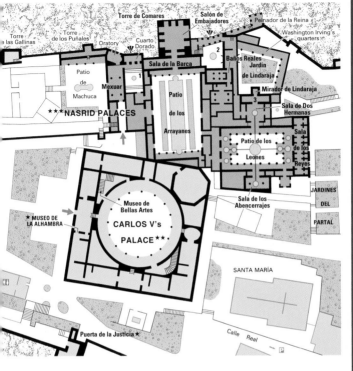

a calligraphic border cover the walls, which are decorated with royal coats of arms. It is thought that this room served an administrative function as a council chamber. Note the small oratory leading off the room to the rear.

Patio del Cuarto Dorado (1) – The magnificent **south wall** is a compendium of Nasrid art. This outstanding wall-façade comprises *azulejos* with geometric decoration, panels with vegetal features, calligraphic borders, a *mocárabe* frieze, a carved wood cornice and a large eave, all of which are arranged around two doors and five windows.

Opposite is the Cuarto Dorado, a wide room with tiled panelling, fine stuccowork and a beautiful wooden ceiling. The **view*** of the Albaicín from its windows is quite magnificent.

Patio de los Arrayanes – The Myrtle Courtyard is reached via a narrow passageway, access to which is through the doorway to the left of the south wall. This delightful rectangular patio has an elongated and narrow pool bordered by myrtle bushes which reflects the massive bulk of the **Torre de Comares**; the latter offers a sharp contrast to the light, slender porticoes

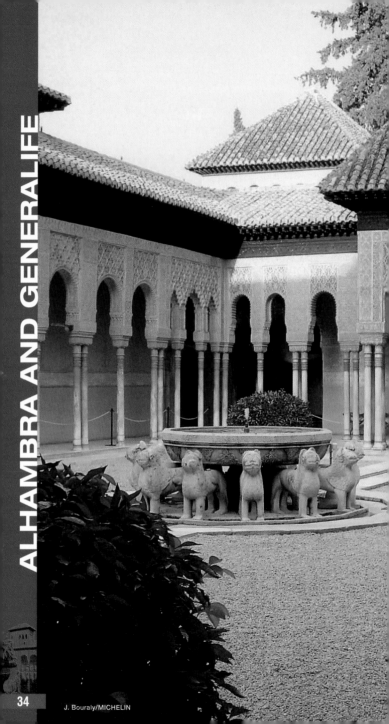

J. Bouraly/MICHELIN

Patio de los Leones

that give onto the **Sala de la Barca**, covered by a magnificent wooden vault with a quarter sphere at each end. The highly decorated walls are adorned with the coats of arms of the Nasrid dynasty and calligraphic inscriptions bearing the words "There is no Saviour but God". This room leads to the **Salón de Embajadores** (Hall of Ambassadors), a square-shaped room used as the audience chamber of the emirs. The richness of its decoration is quite exquisite, with its magnificent lustre *azulejo* panelling, delicate stucco with plant and geometric motifs, and numerous calligraphic strips with religious and poetic inscriptions. The remarkable **dome**, above a line of latticework windows, comprises more than 8 000 pieces of multi-coloured wood and represents the seven heavens of the Koran. Niches on three sides of the room have latticework panels allowing light to filter through.

Patio de los Leones – The justly famous Lion Courtyard dates from the reign of Mohammed V. The 11C fountain of unknown provenance at its centre is supported by 12 rough stone lions, and is surrounded by the delicate arcades of slender columns which lead to the sumptuous main state apartments. Two elegant pavilions supported by columns project over the east and west sides of the courtyard.

The **Sala de los Abencerrajes** on the south side, so called after Boabdil had ordered the massacre of the rival Abencerraje family and piled their heads into the room's central basin, is adorned with a stalactite ceiling and a splendid star-shaped lantern cupola illuminated by 16 windows.

The rectangular **Sala de los Reyes**, or Kings' Chamber, on the east side of the courtyard, comprises three square sections covered with *mocárabe* cupolas, separated by richly ornamented double arches. The painted vaulting adorning the alcoves depicts the pastimes of Moorish and Christian princes and probably dates from the end of the 14C. The style is so atypical that it is not known whether the artist was a Christian working for the Sultan before or after the Reconquest.

The **Sala de Dos Hermanas** (Hall of the Two Sisters), is a square room renowned for its honeycomb dome cupola above an octagon, and its fine *azulejos* and stuccowork. A romantic legend attributes its name to two sisters who were imprisoned within its walls. Beyond are the **Sala de los Ajimeces** and the **Mirador de Lindaraja**, both equally resplendent with their stuccowork and honeycomb decoration. Prior to the construction of Charles V's rooms, the mirador provided views of the outskirts of Granada; nowadays, the panorama is limited to a small garden: the 16C Patio de Lindaraja.

A corridor from the Sala de Dos Hermanas passes the

cupolas of the Royal Baths (*Baños Reales*) to the left, currently closed to visitors. Continue through the room used by the American writer Washington Irving during his period of residence in the Alhambra, to reach an open gallery with delightful **views*** of the Albaicín; descend the stairs to the Patio de la Reja (**2**) and the Patio de Lindaraja.

Cross the Patio de Lindaraja to enter the Jardines del Partal.

Gardens and perimeter towers**

Spreading to the east of the royal palaces are the **Jardines del Partal**, terraced gardens which descend to the towers punctuating the walls. The first tower visible is the **Torre de las Damas** (Ladies' Tower), built by Yusuf I at the beginning of the 14C, and preceded by a graceful *artesonado* portico. The Torre del Mihrab and the former Nasrid mosque (*mezquita*) can be seen to the right. Two further towers, the Torre de la Cautiva (Captive's Tower), also dating from the reign of Yusuf I, and the later Torre de las Infantas (Infantas' Tower), have sumptuous internal decoration.

Enter the Palacio de Carlos V from the Jardines del Partal.

Charles V's palace** (Palacio de Carlos V)

In 1526, Emperor Charles V ordered the construction of this palace which was financed by taxes levied on the *moriscos*. He entrusted the work to **Pedro Machuca**, who had studied in Italy under Michelangelo, and who created a design in pure Classical style. The simplicity of its plan – a circle within a square – and the harmony of its lines endow the building with an unquestionable

H. Champollion/MICHELIN   Carlos V's palace

majestic beauty. The façade comprises two storeys: a lower level of dressed stone, and an upper section adorned with Ionic pilasters.

On the main doorway of the lower level, note the medallions and superb bas-reliefs representing the triumph of peace (at the centre) and military battles (to the side). The upper storey bears the escutcheon of Spain.

The palace's outstanding feature is the large circular patio (31m/102ft in diameter), fronted by Doric columns on the ground floor and Ionic columns on its upper tier. The patio's charm lies in its simplicity and the beauty of its proportions, which combine to create a masterpiece of the Spanish Renaissance.

The palace contains two museums:

Museo de la Alhambra★ – *Entrance to the right of the vestibule.* This pleasant museum is entirely devoted to Hispano-Moorish art and contains exhibits that demonstrate the mastery of the artists and craftsmen from the period. These include ceramics, wood carvings, panels of *azulejos* and *alicatados*, stuccowork, bronzes, fabric etc. Outstanding objects include a 10C ablutions basin, known as the Pila de Almanzor, decorated with lions and stags, the famous **blue or gazelle amphora★**, a delicate 14C masterpiece, the unusual ceramic exhibits representing animals, and replicas of household objects.

Museo de Bellas Artes – *Entrance on the upper storey of the patio.* The Fine Arts Museum contains an interesting collection of paintings and sculptures from the 15C to the 20C. Those from the 15C and 16C include works of a predominantly religious nature by renowned artists

Imagen © TURISMO ANDALUZ S.A.

such as Sánchez Cotán, Siloé, Alonso Cano and Pedro de Mena, in addition to a magnificent still-life, **Thistle and Carrots****, by Sánchez Cotán, which depicts the dignity of the inanimate object with great sobriety; only Zurbarán was equal to this mastery. Both represent the culmination of the Spanish still-life tradition, so austere and so different from that of the great Dutch and Flemish masters.

The rooms devoted to the 19C and 20C contain works by Rodríguez Acosta, Muñoz Degrain, López Mezquita and Manuel Ángeles Ortiz, including a number of more avant-garde exhibits.

Puerta del Vino

The Wine Gateway, built by Mohammed V, may have been erected as a commemorative monument, given its location inside the palace walls and the fact that it did not perform any defensive function. Note the ceramic decoration on the spandrels of the horseshoe arch, and, above it, a paired window flanked by sculpted panels.

Pass through the gateway to reach the Alcazaba.

Alcazaba*

To the left of the Plaza de los Aljibes (Cistern Court), at the westernmost extreme of the palace precinct, stands the Alcazaba, the oldest part of the Alhambra, with its austere, fortress-like appearance, towers and defensive walls. Three of its towers overlook the courtyard: the

Torre del Adarguero, the Torre Quebrada and the Torre del Homenaje (keep). The views of the leafy Alhambra wood from the Jardín de los Adarves on the south side are particularly attractive. The parade ground inside the fortress has preserved some military remains dominated by the imposing bulk of the **Torre de la Vela** (Watchtower), the bulwark on which the Catholic Monarchs hoisted their flags upon their reconquest of Granada. The tower provides a magnificent **panorama**** of the palace, the Generalife, Sacromonte, Granada and the Sierra Nevada. From here, the series of fortifications to the west known as the **Torres Bermejas** (Red Towers), part of the old city's defensive network, can also be seen. Although these were originally built in the late 8C and early 9C, they have been subsequently rebuilt.

Puerta de la Justicia*

Built by Yusuf I, the massive Justice Gateway is built into a tower in the outer walls. The external façade comprises a large horseshoe arch, an inner door, also with a horseshoe arch, and, above it, an inscription and a wide strip of delightful *azulejos* with an image of the Virgin and Child from the early 16C, commissioned by the Catholic Monarchs. The symbolism of the hand on the key of the outer arch and the key and rope on the internal arch remain something of a mystery.

GENERALIFE★★

The name Generalife name derives from the Arabic *Yannat al-Arif*, for which two possible interpretations have been suggested: the "Garden of the Architect" and "the most noble of gardens". It is known that this summer residence already existed in 1319, thus pre-dating the Alhambra Palace. The Generalife consists of a single palace surrounded by magnificent terraced gardens in which running water plays a predominant role once again. The avenue of cypress trees leads to the new gardens, in the centre of which stands an auditorium – the delightful setting for Granada's annual Festival of Music and Dance. The main nucleus of the Generalife is the Patio de la Acequia, a long irrigation pool *(acequia)* lined with water jets and bordered by plants and flowers and with a pavilion at either end; a gallery running along its length has a *mirador* at its centre providing superb views of the Alhambra. The pavilion through the portico to the rear contains the Sala Regia, a room decorated with some fine stuccowork.

The Patio de la Sultana, enclosed on one side by a 16C gallery, owes its names to the so-called **"Sultana's cypress tree"**.

A MEETING-PLACE FOR LOVERS

According to legend, it was by this cypress tree that the wife of the sultan Boabdil and a leader from the rival Abencerraje family would meet. Upon hearing of these secret liaisons, the sultan ordered the well-documented massacre of the members of the Abencerraje family in the room of the palace that now bears their name.

The upper gardens above the palace contain the famous **escalera del agua**, or water staircase, part of a charming scene that highlights the refinements in taste of Moorish culture. Paseo de las Adelfas (Oleander Avenue) and paseo de los Cipreses provide an exit from this haven of tranquillity and greenery.

Exploring
the city

Cathedral quarter★★

allow 2hr

Cathedral★

Entrance on Gran Vía de Colón. ☎ *958 22 29 59.* Construction of the city's cathedral began in 1518 in the middle of the old Moorish city and continued for almost two centuries. The initial project was for a Gothic cathedral similar to that in Toledo. However, the architect Diego Siloé, who replaced Enrique Egas and was entrusted with the project from 1528 until his death in 1563, made changes to the design and introduced the Renaissance style to the building.

Interior – *Entry through the ambulatory.* The interior comprises five sizeable and lofty aisles with adjoining side chapels, and an ambulatory. Enormous square pillars with engaged half columns rise up above elevated pedestals and support large sections of entablature, thereby considerably increasing the overall height. The vaulting above is Gothic in style.

The **chancel★** *(capilla mayor)* is noteworthy for its rich decoration. It is circular in plan with surprising height created by two enormous superimposed orders. In the initial design, the area above the vaulted arches, which connect the chancel with the ambulatory, contained large niches to house royal tombs; these niches were later covered by portraits of Doctors of the Church. The lower order of columns has ledges with statues of Apostles and saints, while the second tier contains seven paintings by Alonso Cano representing scenes from the life of the Virgin Mary. The 16C stained-glass windows above depict scenes from the Gospels, the majority of which are from the Passion. Note also the **silver tabernacle** in the centre of the presbytery.

A large main arch linking the chapel with the aisles houses the statues of the Catholic Monarchs at prayer by Pedro de Mena, and above them two medallions bearing the busts of Adam and Eve, by Alonso Cano. The 18C **organs** between the first two pillars of the nave are particularly impressive.

The right transept arm opens onto the magnificent **north portal of the Royal Chapel★**, dominated by a Virgin and Child. This ornate portal by Enrique Egas is Gothic in style. Above this arch Fernando and Isabel's emblems of the yoke and arrow flank the coat of arms of the Catholic Monarchs. To the left note the large altarpiece dedicated to St James, at the centre of which stands an equestrian statue of the apostle by Alonso de Mena.

Two chapels are worthy of special mention: the **Capilla de la Virgen de las Angustias** and the **Capilla de Nuestra Señora de la Antigua**. The large marble retable of the Virgin of An-

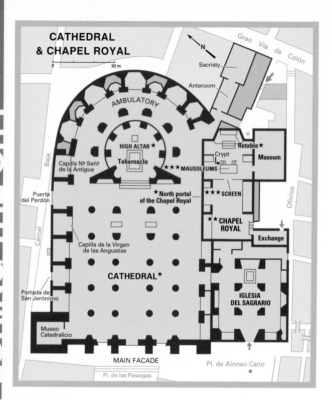

CATHEDRAL & CHAPEL ROYAL

N

0   30 m

Sacristy

Anteroom

AMBULATORY

Baja

HIGH ALTAR ★

Retable ★

Museum

Capilla Nª Señª
de la Antigua

Tabernacle

Crypt

★★★ MAUSOLEUMS

Puerta
del Perdón

★ North portal
of the Chapel Royal

★★★ SCREEN

Oficios

Cárcel

★★ CHAPEL
ROYAL

Capilla de la Virgen
de las Angustias

Exchange

Portada de
San Jerónimo

CATHEDRAL ★

IGLESIA
DEL SAGRARIO

Museo
Catedralicio

MAIN FACADE

Pl. de Alonso Cano

Pl. de las Pasiegas

Gran Vía de Colón

guish *(angustias)* was housed in the retrochoir until 1926. At its centre the Virgin appears with the dead Christ in her arms and accompanied by several saints. The chapel of Nuestra Señora de la Antigua contains a fine 15C statue of this particular Virgin and Child at the centre of a magnificent early-18C Baroque altarpiece by Pedro Duque Cornejo. The ambulatory contains an interesting collection of choir books from the 16C to 18C.

The **Museo Catedralicio** has several notable exhibits, including a small image of the Virgin of Bethlehem, a bust of St Paul by Alonso Cano, and

a bust of the Virgin and Child by Pedro de Mena.

Another delightful image of the Virgin, by Alonso Cano, can be seen at Christ's feet in the **sacristy**.

Exterior – Continue around the apse and exit the cathedral onto calle Cárcel Baja, where two doorways designed by Siloé can be seen. The lower section of the **Puerta del Perdón** (Pardon Doorway) is another example of his architectural genius, on which the figures of Faith and Justice appear against the arch, holding a tablet. Two magnificent escutcheons, one of the Catholic Monarchs *(to the left)*, the other of Emperor

Charles V *(to the right)* adorn the buttresses. The **Portada de San Jerónimo**, a portal named in honour of St Jerome, has a semicircular arch between Plateresque pilasters and medallions with cherubim in the spandrels of the arch. Above the arch, note the relief of a penitent St Jerome.

The main monumental façade overlooking the plaza de las Pasiegas was designed by Alonso Cano in 1667.

Madraza
or Ayuntamiento Viejo

In calle Oficios, opposite the Royal Chapel. The Madraza (Muslim University) was built in the 14C by Yusuf I. Following the Reconquest, the Catholic Monarchs requisitioned the building for use as Granada's former city hall *(ayuntamiento viejo)*. The façade, late Granada Baroque in style, was created in the 18C, when the building was practically rebuilt. The decoration is mainly confined to the large balconies on the upper floor. An escutcheon between these balconies completes the decorative work.

Inside, across the inner patio, stands the former Moorish **oratory**, an attractive hall of polychrome stuccowork, *mocárabe* decoration and a delightful octagonal dome adorned with a lantern.

Capilla Real★★

☎ *958 22 92 39.* The Catholic Monarchs ordered the construction of the Royal Chapel with the express intention of being buried in the city that had bathed them in such glory. They entrusted the building work to the architect Enrique Egas, who commenced the project in 1506 and completed it 15 years later. It is a masterpiece of the Isabelline Gothic style, both in terms of its stylistic unity and the richness of its ornamentation.

The outstanding features of the **exterior** are the fine pinnacles and elegant **cresting**, the lower section of which is decorated with the letters F and Y, representing the initials of the Catholic Monarchs. The main doorway of the chapel was incorporated inside the cathedral upon the construction of the latter. Access is via the old Lonja (Exchange).

The **Lonja** is a graceful 16C Plateresque building with a rectangular ground plan and two floors. Decorative columns, adorned with spheres and spiral cord decoration, support the arches. The coat of arms of the city is emblazoned on the lower section. The upper floor gallery contains the emblems of the Catholic Monarchs and Charles V on the carved sills.

A HISTORIC PLACE OF REST

The importance of the reign of the **Catholic Monarchs** cannot be underestimated, with their influence extending far beyond the Iberian Peninsula. This was particularly true of the discovery of America, to which they had given their financial and political support. Their marriage was also to have a determining effect on the history of Spain, by uniting the kingdoms of Castilla and Aragón into a political and geographical entity that would provide the basis for the future Spanish state and bring the country into the modern age. However, their reign is overshadowed by less glorious events, including the expulsion of Jews from the country and the establishment of the Spanish Inquisition.

The **interior** consists of a single nave with side chapels, with ribbed vaults supported by pillars with large bead moulding. A blue fringe with a gilded inscription adorns the upper part of the walls. However, the most characteristic decoration inside the Royal Chapel is the profusion of heraldic features with the coats of arms and emblems of the Catholic Monarchs on the walls and wrought-iron grilles.

A spectacular 16C **screen***** by Master Bartolomé of Jaén encloses the chancel. In the centre, note the escutcheon and yoke and arrow emblems of Fernando and Isabel, in addition to the scenes of the life of Christ on the upper section.

The two double **mausoleums***** in the chancel, one of the Catholic Monarchs, the other of their daughter, Juana la Loca (Joan the Mad), and her husband, Felipe el Hermoso (Philip the Handsome), are quite outstanding. The first, the work of the Tuscan sculptor Domenico Fancelli, was carved in Genoa in 1517 from Carrara marble, and is decorated with reliefs of Apostles and medallions; those in the middle represent the baptism and resurrection of Christ. The upper part reveals the sculptures of the monarchs above angels bearing an escutcheon-adorned garland. Their epitaph is engraved on the tablet at the base of the mausoleum. The second, equally impressive mausoleum is a work carved by Bartolomé Ordóñez in 1519 on a pedestal decorated with religious scenes. The sarcophagus above it is topped by the recumbent statues of Juana and Felipe.

The royal remains are contained in four simple coffins in the chapel's crypt.

The magnificent Plateresque **retable*** at the high altar was sculpted by Felipe Vigarny between 1520 and 1522. The artist has succeeded in endowing his figures with energetic movement and great expression. The scene is dominated by a crucified Christ accompanied by the Virgin Mary and St John. The lower register of the predella depicts the siege of Granada and the baptism of the *moriscos*. Note also the praying statues of the Catholic Monarchs attributed to Diego de Siloé.

Museum – *Access by the north arm of the transept.* Numerous objects of incalculable historical value can be seen in this museum which is housed in the sacristy. Among the exhibits on display are **Queen Isabel's sceptre and crown**, **King Fernando's sword**, plus an outstanding **collection of paintings**** by Flemish (Rogier van der Weyden, Memling), Italian (Perugino, Botticelli) and Spanish (Bartolomé Bermejo, Pedro Berruguete) artists. In the rear of the museum can be found the famous **Triptych of the Passion** by the Fleming Dirk Bouts and two sculptures of the Catholic Monarchs at prayer by Felipe Vigarny.

Curia

The doorway of this 16C Plateresque-style building is adorned with an archiepiscopal escutcheon on its semicircular pediment. To the left stands the **Palacio Arzobispal**, or Archbishop's Palace, of simple design.

Bouraly/MICHELIN

Side wall of the cathedral

Iglesia del Sagrario

This 18C church was built on the site of the city's main mosque. It is known that the architect Francisco Hurtado Izquierdo was involved in its design.

Plaza Bib-Rambla

This attractive rectangular square in the centre of the city is the setting for a number of colourful flower stalls. The plaza is further embellished by attractive street-lamps and a large central fountain crowned by Neptune.

Alcaicería

In Moorish times the area was occupied by the city's silk market. It has now been rebuilt and transformed into a market for craft and souvenir shops. The Alcaicería still retains its Moorish atmosphere thanks to its narrow alleyways, horseshoe arches and Arabic-style decoration.

Corral del Carbón

This former storehouse is a Moorish construction dating from the 14C. It has a harmonious doorway with a horseshoe arch adorned with an *alfiz* surround and above it an inscription and a paired window flanked by two panels with *sebka* decoration. The doorway is crowned by a large wooden eave, while the portico is topped by *mocárabe* vaulting.

The sober internal patio is of particular interest with its three storeys of straight galleries supported by brick pillars with wooden capitals, and a simple fountain at its centre, all of which combine to create a charming scene.

Casa de los Duques de Abrantes

In placeta Tovar, to the left of the Corral del Carbón. This 16C building has a simple Gothic-influenced doorway with heraldic decoration.

Plaza de Isabel la Católica

The square is dominated by the Monument to the Santa Fe Agreement (1892), a work by Mariano Benlliure, in which Columbus is depicted presenting his plans to Queen Isabel.

Casa de los Tiros

Built in the mid-16C, this palace has an unusual stone façade with just five, almost round, sculptures of figures in warrior-like attire. It now houses the city's newspaper and periodicals library (Hemeroteca).

Plaza Bib-Rambla and the cathedral

Carrera del Darro ★

allow 1hr

This delightful street, which is bordered by the River Darro, runs from plaza de Santa Ana to paseo de los Tristes. The walk along carrera del Darro leaves the modern city behind and enters an area with a completely different appearance in which the atmosphere is more akin to a village or small town than a large city. The street skirts the right bank of the river which is spanned by several simple stone bridges providing access to Granada's legendary hills, the Alhambra and Albaicín.

Before starting the walk, several buildings in **plaza Nueva** and **plaza de Santa Ana** are worthy of special interest.

Chancillería

The former chancery now houses Andalucía's High Court of Justice. This 16C building on plaza Nueva has a Classical façade, characterised by a combination of various architectural elements which already show Baroque undertones in their design. The marble doorway is dominated by a large Spanish coat of arms. The balustrade crowning the building

Imagen © TURISMO ANDALUZ S.A.

The Chancel

was added in the 18C. The delightful and harmonious **patio***, attributed to Siloé, is particularly attractive.

Iglesia de Santa Ana y San Gil

Plaza de Santa Ana. This small 16C church was built according to plans by Diego de Siloé. The handsome bell tower has colourful *azulejo* decoration on the arch spandrels and pinnacle section. The church portal is decorated with three niches bearing statues of St Anne and two additional female saints and a medallion of the Virgin and Child. The main features of the interior are the Mudéjar-style ceilings above the nave and chancel.

A 16C fountain, the **Pilar del Toro**, also attributed to Siloé, can be seen in the same square. It is adorned with the coat of arms of the city above a relief of a bull's head that has lent the fountain its name.

Follow carrera del Darro.

El Bañuelo*

(Moorish baths)

☎ 958 02 78 00. The Moorish baths are situated opposite the remains of the 11C bridge known as the **Puente del Cadí**, of which only a part of a fortified tower and a horseshoe arch remain.

Built in the 11C, they have a typically Moorish structure and comprise several rooms (changing areas, a meeting and massage room, and the baths themselves). Note the star-pierced vaulting with octagonal skylights and the arcades in the last two rooms with Roman, Caliphal and Visigothic capitals. Despite their age, the baths are some of the best preserved in Spain.

The towers and walls of the Alhambra are visible from here.

Convento de Santa Catalina de Zafra

This 16C convent has a Renaissance-type doorway with a semicircular arch framed by pilasters and with medallions on the spandrels. Above it sits a niche housing a statue of the saint flanked by two coats of arms.

Casa Castril

The city's **archaeological museum** *(see description under "Monuments and sights of interest")* is housed in the Casa Castril (1539), fronted by a fine **Plateresque doorway***, profusely decorated with heraldic motifs, scallop-shells, animals, figures etc.

Iglesia de San Pedro

Opposite the museum. The 16C Church of St Peter occupies an attractive location on the banks of the Darro, watched over by the Comares Tower *(torre)*. Two sculptures dominate its simple portal: the figure of St Peter holding the keys, and St Paul clasping a sword.

Paseo de los Tristes

Carrera del Darro runs into this avenue, which offers superb **views*** of the Alhambra, with its towers and walls emerging from the greenery of the hill. The panorama from here is particularly impressive at night, when the palace is illuminated. Small café terraces provide the perfect setting from which to admire this memorable sight.

Albaicín ★★ *allow 1hr 30min*

This district, which has lent its name to the hill on which it stands, is Granada's most famous quarter, offering magnificent views of the Alhambra at every turn. It was here that the first Moorish fortress was built in the city, although only the walls survive from this early construction. A maze of narrow alleyways wind their way up the hill between the palisades of small villas known as *cármenes*, through delightful small squares and past picturesque street corners. The Albaicín is best explored on foot in order to fully appreciate the heritage of this Moorish section of the city.

Palacio de los Córdova
At the foot of the cuesta del Chapiz. An avenue of cypress trees in the garden leads to the palace, its Renaissance doorway adorned with heraldic decoration. The building is now home to the Municipal Archives.

Casa del Chapiz
Entrance along camino de Sacromonte. The mansion is now the headquarters of the School of Arabic Studies. The complex is a combination of two Moorish houses from the 15C and 16C with patios and galleries. The gardens offer pleasant **views*** of the Alhambra.

Delve deeper into the Albaicín along cuesta de San Agustín, which climbs between the typical *cármenes* and provides a first glimpse of the Alhambra.

Mirador de San Nicolás
This terrace in front of the **Iglesia de San Nicolás** enjoys one of the best **views***** of Granada's magnificent backdrop, encompassing the breathtaking beauty of the ochre-coloured Alhambra standing out against its verdant hillside, and the superb outline of the Sierra Nevada. *Pass in front of the church and follow the callejón de San Cecilio to the end, then turn right and continue through the Arco de las Pesas.*

Arco de las Pesas
This simple 11C arch, standing alongside the pleasant plaza Larga, was part of the walls of the old fortress. It has a typically Moorish structure with an angled entrance. *Return through the arch. From plaza de Minas, head along cuesta de María de la Miel, then turn right onto camino Nuevo de San Nicolás.*

Convento de Santa Isabel la Real
Enter the doorway of this monastery founded by Isabel the Catholic at the beginning

---

CÁRMENES

This is the name given to the small villas found in the Albaicín. They are a more modern version of a type of Moorish residence or *carmen* which would have consisted of a house and its adjoining kitchen garden *(huerto)*.

Backstreets of the Albayzín district

of the 16C to admire the church's fine, pinnacled Gothic portal bearing the coat of arms and yoke and arrow emblems of the Catholic Monarchs. The interior contains some fine Mudéjar decoration.

Plaza de San Miguel Bajo

A Christ of the Lanterns adorns this square, which is fronted by the church that has lent it its name.

Follow the street opposite the church. At the end of this street, the lower town comes into view.

Turn left and left again along calle Bocanegra, then right along calle San José.

Iglesia de San José

The church was built in the 16C above the former mosque. The 10C minaret from this earlier building still remains, although it has now been converted into a bell tower.

Imagen © TURISMO ANDALUZ S.A.

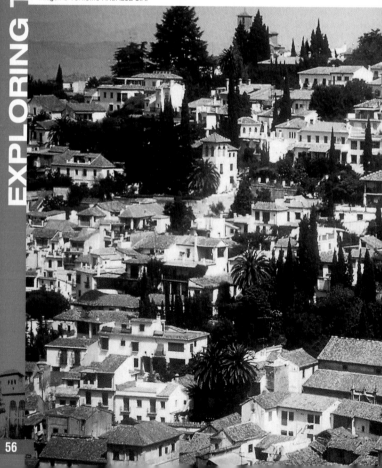

Continue heading down, then look to the right immediately after some steps.

Casa de Porras

This mansion is fronted by a simple stone doorway with heraldic decoration.

A delightful typical villa, the Carmen de los Cipreses (cypress trees), can be seen opposite. The trees that have given the house its name are visible from the street.

Head down cuesta del Granadillo and the extremely narrow cuesta Aceituneros to emerge at the start of carrera del Darro, opposite the Iglesia de Santa Ana y San Gil.

MIRADOR DE SAN CRISTÓBAL

This *mirador* along the Carretera de Murcia offers a superb **view***★* of the Albaicín with its typical villas or *cármenes*, the walls of the old fortress in the foreground, the Alhambra in the background and the lower town to the right.

View over the picturesque district of Albayzín

From the University to the Royal Hospital★

allow 1hr

This district of the city contains a number of interesting 17C and 18C churches and civic monuments.

University

This Baroque building, the seat of the city's university from the 18C onwards, is situated on plaza de la Universidad; the statue of its founder, Charles V, stands proudly in the centre of the square. The building, its façade embellished by Solomonic columns, is now home to the university's Faculty of Law.

Iglesia de los Santos Justo y Pastor

On the same square. The lower section of the church's 18C Baroque portal includes the reliefs of St Francis Xavier and St Francis Borgia, along with the coat of arms of the Society of Jesus above the arch; the upper tier bears a large relief depicting the conversion of St Paul.

The wall paintings on the interior are of interest, particularly those of the saints between the windows of the cupola tambour above the transept.

Colegio de San Bartolomé y Santiago

This college dates from 1621. To the left of the simple doorway, adorned with Doric columns and the sculptures of the college's patron saints, the large cupola of the Iglesia de los Santos Justo y Pastor is visible. It is well worth entering the elegant patio with its slender Doric columns and basket-handle arches.

From the corner of calle de la Duquesa and Gran Capitán, admire the monumental **apse** in the church of the **Monasterio de San Jerónimo★** *(see description under "Monuments and sights of interest").*

The **Hospital de San Juan de Dios** in calle San Juan de Dios was built between the 16C and 18C.

Iglesia de San Juan de Dios★

Built in the first half of the 18C, this church is one of Granada's principal Baroque churches. The richly ornamented **façade★** comprises a portal enclosed between bell towers topped with spires. The niches on the lower section contain images of the archangels Gabriel and

Raphael; the central part of the upper section shows the patron saint of the church accompanied by reliefs of St Ildefonsus and St Barbara.

The **interior**, access to which is via a beautiful carved mahogany doorway, has a Latin-cross ground plan with side chapels, an elevated cupola above the transept and a chancel. It is magnificent in both its richness and its stylistic uniformity. The high altar is dominated by a massive Churrigueresque altarpiece of gilded wood behind which is hidden a chapel *(camarín)* whose doors are normally closed. This **camarín** is accessed via a door to the right of the altar. It consists of three lavish rooms ornamented in the most decorative of Baroque styles.

The middle room houses the tabernacle with the urn containing the remains of the saint – the founder of the Order of Hospitallers, who died in 1550. The walls, awash with gilded wood, are full of reliquaries of saints.

Monumento a la Inmaculada Concepción

This 17C monument to the Immaculate Conception stands in the attractive **Jardines del Triunfo** (Triumph Gardens). The statue of a crowned Virgin Mary surrounded by beams of light on top of the column is by Alonso de Mena. The side walls of the Royal Hospital are visible behind the monument.

Hospital Real

The former Royal Hospital was founded by the Catholic Monarchs at the beginning of the 16C and is now home to the university Rectorate. The celebrated architect Enrique Egas was responsible for the first stage of its construction. In keeping with other hospitals, such as those in Toledo and Santiago de Compostela, the ground plan is of a cross within a square and four inner patios. Four Plateresque windows adorn the façade's upper storey. The entablature above the 17C marble doorway is decorated with the yoke and arrow – the emblems of the Catholic Monarchs; above it sits a Virgin and Child, flanked by the statues of Fernando and Isabel at prayer. The sculptures are the work of Alonso de Mena.

Of interest in the interior are the two patios in the left wing, decorated with heraldic motifs.

From the first patio to the right, stairs lead to the university's central library (bibloteca central), which occupies the large room on the first floor. The library has an open framework and a wooden coffered dome above squinch arches at its centre.

Monuments
and sights
of interest

Monasterio de San Jerónimo★

VISIT

Entrance on calle López de Argueta. ☎ *958 27 93 37.*

Construction of the monastery began in 1496. Two celebrated architects worked on the building: Jacopo Fiorentino, also known as Jacopo l'Indaco, until 1526, and Diego Siloé, after this date.

After crossing the atrium, note the **façade** of the church before entering the monastic buildings. The upper section, bearing the coats of arms of the Catholic Monarchs, has a fine window flanked by medallions and grotesque animal figures.

Enter the monastery.

The large **cloisters**, with a garden of orange trees at its centre, were completed in 1519 according to plans principally designed by Diego de Siloé. Robust pillars with foliated capitals support semicircular arches on the lower tier and basket-handle arches on the upper register. Another characteristic feature of the cloisters is the plethora of Plateresque and Renaissance doorways opening onto it. A stroll around the patio reveals the impressive wall of the church, with its handsome Plateresque window and the magnificent and monumental escutcheon of El Gran Capitán.

Church★★

The scene greeting the visitor through the fine Siloé-designed **Plateresque doorway** from the cloisters is quite a surprise, such is the rich decoration inside: vaults and domes with high reliefs, a magnificent main retable and paintings on the walls, all of which combine to create a masterpiece of Spanish Renaissance architecture.

Construction of the church began during the period of Gothic influence, although the transept and apse were completed during the Renaissance, once Siloé assumed responsibility for the work. The widow of Gonzalo Fernández de Córdoba financed the building for the purpose of creating a mausoleum for her husband, El Gran Capitán.

Attention is first drawn to the richness of the apse, superbly illuminated by the transept windows, and the dome, with its fan vaulting and double arches with caissons decorated with busts; the squinch arches contain the statues of the four Evangelists. The coffered vaulting above the transept arms is decorated with high reliefs of biblical characters, angels, animals etc, while the vault above the high altar depicts

Christ accompanied by Apostles, angels and saints. The large **retable****, worked on by a number of artists, is a jewel of the Granadine School. It portrays saints, scenes from the life of the Virgin Mary and Christ, as well as a depiction of God the Father above some clouds on the crowning piece. The statues of El Gran Capitán and his wife at prayer are to the side, while a simple stone slab marks the burial place of Don Gonzalo. The paintings decorating the walls of the church were added in the 18C.

B. Kaufmann/MICHELIN

Detail, the church façade

S·PEDRO

$\mathcal{L}$a Cartuja ★

☎ 958 16 19 32 (10am-noon).

Construction of the Carthusian monastery began at the beginning of the 16C. Entry is through a Plateresque portal leading into the large atrium, at the end of which is the church and other outbuildings belonging to the monastery, which can be reached through the cloisters.

The façade of the church is simple in style, with the shield of Spain visible at the top and a statue of St Bruno presiding over the portal.

Some of the outbuildings house paintings by Sánchez Cotán and Vicente Carducho, both of whom were Carthusian monks in the monastery.

Church – The church is exuberantly decorated with Baroque stucco (1662) and paintings. The nave is divided into three sections (for the monks, lay brothers and public). The areas for the monks and lay brothers are separated by a gilded screen with richly decorated doors and paintings on either side by Sánchez Cotán: *The Baptism of Christ* and *Rest after the Flight into Egypt*.

The Assumption, which is visible below the baldaquin, is the work of José de Mora. Behind it is the **sacrarium**, a *camarín* decorated at the beginning of the 18C by Francisco Hurtado Izquierdo, whose style, polychrome colours and materials are all extravagantly Baroque, resulting in a decorative exuberance which is almost oppressive.

Sacristy★★ – Built between 1727 and 1764, this is one of the masterpieces of the Spanish Baroque period. The architectural elements are disguised by a rich decoration of white stucco, mixtilinear mouldings and cornices which are broken in numerous places to extraordinary effect. The strong daylight which filters through the windows emphasises the play of light and shadow created by this lavish decor. Above the apse, the dark fresco paintings of the oval cupola contrast sharply with the white stucco ornamentation elsewhere in the church. Lanjarón marble is used extensively in the room, as well as for the altarpieces of the saints in the apse. The magnificent door and the cedarwood furnishings inlaid with tortoiseshell, mother-of-pearl and silver, are by a Carthusian monk, Brother José Manuel Vázquez.

*O*ther places of interest

Museo Arqueológico

☎ *958 22 56 40*. The archaeological museum is housed in the Casa Castril (1539), a Renaissance palace with a fine **Plateresque doorway***. Exhibits include an interesting collection of 9C BC Egyptian alabaster vases, discovered at a Punic necropolis in Almuñécar, a bull figure from Arjona, and numerous Roman artefacts and Moorish decorative objects. The museum also has a copy of the *Dama de Baza*, the original of which is on display in the Museo Arqueológico Nacional in Madrid.

Sacromonte

The hill of Sacromonte (literally "sacred mountain") rises alongside the Albaicín quarter, opposite the Generalife.

Imagen © TURISMO ANDALUZ S.A.

Flamenco shows are frequently staged in some of the cave dwellings in this gypsy troglodyte district, which is now partially abandoned.

Casa-Museo Manuel de Falla

☎ *958 22 94 21*. The composer Manuel de Falla (1876-1946), a passionate admirer of Granada although he only came to know the city after the age of 40, lived in this 16C house between 1919 and 1939. The house of the composer of such famous works as *Love, the Magician* and *The Three-Cornered Hat* is unchanged since the days when he lived here. The piano, guitar and furniture of this exceptional musician provide visitors with an insight into his professional and private lives.

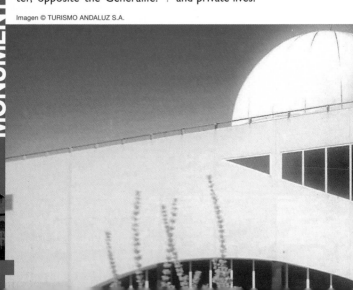

Carmen de los Mártires

☎ *958 22 79 53.* The Carmelite monastery is situated on the Alhambra hill. The luxuriant terraced **gardens**★ are open to the public and provide a beautiful setting for a stroll, with their Romantic 19C decor of fountains and statues and views of the city. Next to the building is a Moorish-style garden and portico.

Iglesia de Santo Domingo

This 16C church stands in the plaza de Santo Domingo. It is mainly Renaissance in style, although the building also retains some Gothic features. The façade is decorated with an elegant stone portico comprising three semicircular arches, whose spandrels are adorned with the initials of the Catholic Monarchs, their shield and that of the Emperor Charles V. A beautiful twin window can be seen above the portico.

Parque de las Ciencias★

☎ *958 13 19 00.* The aim of this large science park is to provide visitors with a better understanding of the world in which they live. In addition to its interactive museum, the complex houses a planetarium, an astronomical observatory and a tropical butterfly collection.

Adults and children alike will enjoy learning from and interacting with the various exhibits on display. A special area, Explora, has been set aside for very young visitors (aged three to seven).

Huerta de San Vicente

☎ *958 25 84 66.* Fans of Federico García Lorca (1898-1936), one of the greatest of Spanish poets and writers, will enjoy this visit to his summer home. The house is situated in the Parque García Lorca, which until recently was no more than a fertile plain; it has been set out exactly as it would have been when Federico used to come here to spend the summer.

Parque de las Ciencias

Excursions

Alcalá la Real★

54km/34mi NW of Granada along the N 432. This attractive town is situated in the southern half of Jaén province, close to the Parque Natural de la Sierra Subbética (to the west).

🄷 *Paseo de los Álamos, Fortaleza de la Mota,* ☎ *953 58 22 17.*

Alcalá la Real stands amid an undulating landscape carpeted in extensive olive groves, overlooked by the Fortaleza de la Mota, an imposing fortress offering magnificent views of the surrounding area.

The birthplace of the poet Juan Ruiz, known as the **Arcipreste de Hita**, and the medieval sculptors **Juan Martínez Montañés** and **Pablo de Rojas**, Alcalá is nowadays an active agricultural and commercial centre with numerous shops, most of which are concentrated

A BORDER TOWN

The town's origins date back to prehistoric times; however, due to its strategic position on the border between Christian- and Muslim-held lands, it became synonymous with fierce battles between the two adversaries. During the period of Moorish domination, which lasted over 600 years, *Qalat*, (a fortified settlement in Arabic), as it was then known, reached the pinnacle of its splendour, until its reconquest by Alfonso XI in 1341.

J. Bouraly/MICHELIN

along calle San Fernando. Typical local dishes include *pollo a la secretaria*, a chicken dish with peppers, peas and an onion and saffron sauce.

Fortaleza de la Mota★★

The fortress enjoys a majestic site on the hill of the same name. It is difficult to distinguish the crags and rocks from the castle walls, which have preserved their seven entrance gates. The Puerta de la Imagen, very similar in appearance to the Puerta de la Justicia in the Alhambra (Granada), is particularly worthy of note.

The fortress is divided into two sections dating from different periods: the Moorish *alcazaba* and the abbey churches. The first is a castle with three towers: the Torre de Mocha, Torre de la Campana and Torre del Homenaje. Inside the castle, built on the remains of the former mosque, stands the **Iglesia de Santo Domingo★**, a Gothic-Mudéjar church built by Alfonso XI. It has preserved the tower of the former minaret – one of the most characteristic features of Alcalá – as well as a fine 15C retable. The **Iglesia de Santa María la Mayor** can be seen on an esplanade of the fortress. Badly damaged during the War of Independence, it has, nevertheless, retained an attractive Renaissance **façade**, Plateresque in style, on which Diego de Siloé is known to have worked. This monumental complex also houses the interesting **Museo**

Fortaleza de la Mota with amazing views over the countryside

Arqueológico, inside the Torre del Homenaje, with its collection of archaeological exhibits from Alcalá and the surrounding locality.

Iglesia de Nuestra Señora de las Angustias

This impressive, octagonal church built by Ventura Rodríguez in the 13C contains an exceptional set of medieval painted wooden **tablets*** and the font where the artists Martínez Montañés and de Rojas were baptised.

Ayuntamiento

The town hall, situated on the pleasant **plaza del Arcipreste de Hita**, occupies a charming 18C Baroque building flanked by two towers. Opposite stands an artistic **sundial*** by Fernando Tapia.

Palacio Abacial

The abbot's palace, in front of the attractive Los Álamos fountain at one end of the paseo of the same name *(see below)*, is housed in a sober neo-Classical building, the façade of which has a Renaissance-inspired balcony and an elegant doorway with reliefs and coats of arms of noble families.

Paseo de los Álamos

This delightful avenue is the ideal place to relax at the end of a long day and enjoy a chilled glass of the local wine on the outdoor terraces of its numerous tapas bars.

R. Mattes/MICHELIN

Fortaleza de la Mota, Alcalá la Real

Around Alcalá la Real

Castillo de Locubín

12km/8mi N along the J 2340.
The road winds its way to the Puerto del Castillo pass, the setting for this small, white-washed settlement, with its superb **views*** of the River San Juan and Víboras Reservoir *(embalse)*. It is worth visiting the remains of the old **Moorish castle** which, along with the fortresses at Alcaudete and Alcalá la Real, was part of the defensive system on the border with the kingdom occupied by the Moors.

Alcaudete

26km/16mi NW along the N 432. Alcaudete is nestled in the folds of a small promontory, hidden amid olive groves. It was conquered by the Infante Don Fernando de Antequera in 1408, from which time it became one of the most important points along the border with the kingdom of Granada. It is renowned for its pastries: *hojaldrinas,* cider *empanadillas* and *roscos de vino*, doughnut-like cakes made by the nuns from the Convento de Santa Clara.

Castle ruins – The Moorish *alcazaba* was built on the site of a former Roman fortress and has preserved several vestiges of its walls and keep.

Iglesia de Santa María – The solemn silhouette of this Gothic church with its Plateresque side portal stands at the foot of the castle. Inside the church, note the fine coffered **artesonado ceiling**, the Renaissance grilles in front of the high altar, and the doors of the sacristy.

Iglesia de San Pedro – This 16C Mudéjar-style church contains an interesting altarpiece.

Plaza Mayor – The main square is situated at the heart of a labyrinth of narrow streets with a number of shops and bars. The 18C town hall comes into view after passing through an archway known as the Arco de la Villa.

Alhama de Granada ★

In the far west of the province, on the banks of the River Alhama, 60km/37mi SW of Granada along the A 338.
🛈 *Paseo Montes Jovellar, ☎ 958 36 06 86.*

Alhama de Granada is one of Andalucía's most attractive small towns, with its whitewashed houses and narrow streets. Its location, literally hanging above a gorge, has inspired poets and travellers alike through the centuries. The Moors named it Al-Hamma, meaning "hot spring", due to the thermal waters found here. Its renown was such that during the period of the Reconquest, Christians paid enormous sums of money to take the waters here.

Moorish quarter★

Alhama has preserved an interesting Moorish quarter which can be easily explored on foot. A viewpoint behind the **Iglesia del Carmen** provides an pleasant introduction to the town with its impressive **view**★ over the famous gorge of the River Alhama. Walk around the church to the delightful Baroque Capilla de Jesús Nazareno, passing an old Arab fortress which was extensively restored in the 19C. Head up calle Baja de la Iglesia until you reach the imposing tower of the **Iglesia de la Encarnación**, which rises above the neighbouring whitewashed houses.

Iglesia de la Encarnación★ – The church, whose name symbolises the incarnation of the Christian faith over Islam, is built above a former mosque, several stones of which can still be distinguished on the south façade. The Baroque portal conceals an early Gothic façade decorated with plant motifs and fantastic animals. The single-nave interior is somewhat sober in style and topped by a complex pointed vault. The sacristy contains a small museum in which a set of valuable 16C priests' garments *(ternos)* are the prize exhibits.

Upon leaving the church, admire the **Casa de la Inquisición** *(to the right)*, an Isabelline Gothic-style building used as a House of the

---

A VALUABLE PRIZE

Alhama was captured from the Moors by Christian troops under the Castilian leader **Ponce de León** in 1482, signalling the start of the **War of Granada**, which ended with the capture of the Nasrid capital ten years later. Due to its magnificent, almost impregnable position, the fertile fields surrounding it and, above all, its springs of thermal water, the qualities of which have been known since Roman times, Alhama was considered one of the jewels in the Nasrid crown. As such, its capture by the Christians was a mighty blow.

Inquisition. It was demolished and subsequently rebuilt in the 1950s. The enchanting plaza de los Presos can be seen on the other side of the tower with, to the right, the former 17C **prison**, and opposite, the well-preserved façade of the 16C **granary**. Calle Vendederas leads to what was once the kingdom of Granada's first military field hospital, built in 1485, and now housing the town's **tourist office**.

Walk around the outside of the tourist office and follow calle Caño Wamba. Here, an unusual 16C fountain can be seen, along with the ruins of the **Iglesia de las Angustias** a little further along the street.

Head down calle de la Mina as far as the so-called Moorish dungeons (mazmorras árabes). These cavities, excavated out of the rock, were used in the past as both a prison and as silos for grain.

B. Kaufmann/MICHELIN

Moorish cistern

Las Alpujarras ★★

The Alpujarras (from the Arabic *al-bucharrat* meaning 'pastures') is a region of small whitewashed villages, rugged mountains and fertile valleys straddled across the provinces of Granada and Almería. Because of its isolation and rugged landscape, it was to be the setting for two of Andalucía's key historical events: it was the final stronghold of the Nasrids following the Christian conquest of Granada, and the focal point of a rebellion by the *moriscos* in 1568. A backwater for three centuries, this magnificent mountain range was subsequently rediscovered by 19C Romantic travellers, and today has developed into one of Andalucía's most popular tourist destinations. Despite this influx of visitors, it has still managed to preserve many of its charms, customs and traditions.

This rugged region extends east to west across the southern slopes of the Sierra Nevada, bordered by the Sierra de la Contraviesa to the south and the Parque Nacional de Sierra Nevada to the north. The suggested itinerary below starts in Lanjarón, 51km/32mi S of Granada via the A 44 motorway and A 348.

🚺 *Lanjarón: Avenida de la Alpujarra, ☎ 958 77 02 82.*

Centro de Interpretación del Parque Nacional de Sierra Nevada (NEVADENSIS) – Pampaneira: Plaza de la Libertad, ☎ 958 76 31 27. The Sierra Nevada Information Centre organises activities such as hikes through the Alpujarras, ascents
of the Sierra Nevada, descents of mountain ravines and horse trekking.

Centro de Información del Puerto de la Ragua – at Km 1 on the Puerto de la Ragua road, ☎ 958 34 55 28. Activities including cross-country skiing and dog-sleigh excursions can be arranged at this information centre; www.laragua.net

From Lanjarón to Bayárcal: 100km/62mi (127km/79mi including the excursion to Puerto de la Ragua) – allow 2 days.

Lanjarón

Lanjarón acts as a natural entrance to the area from Granada and is one of the most accessible towns in the Alpujarras. Famous for its medicinal mineral water, it has developed into a popular tourist base, attracting thousands of visitors every year. In addition to its famed waters, the town's other main attraction is its 16C **castle**, guarding the entrance to the valley from its superb elevated position.

The A 348 road offers magnificent views of the arid and imposing Sierra de Lújar.

9km/5.5mi from Lanjarón, before reaching the town of Órgiva, take the GR 421, which crosses the northern stretch of the Alpujarras. Caution is required when driving along this narrow mountain road.

Before reaching Pampaneira, the road passes through three small villages, **Cañar**, with its impressive views, Carataunas and Soportújar, none of which are on the main tourist track.

Pampaneira**

Leave your car in the car park at the entrance to the town, then continue on foot. Pampaneira is the first of the three villages in the **Poqueira Valley****. Although recently discovered by tourists, it has still managed to preserve its traditional atmosphere. The main street, with its myriad shops selling local products, leads to the **plaza de la Libertad**, dominated by the 17C Baroque Iglesia de la Santa Cruz. The best way

Backstreet, Pampaneira

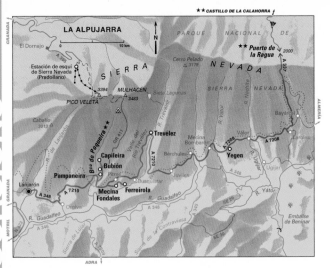

of discovering the charms of these villages is to wander through their narrow streets. In Pampaneira, a number of traditional looms producing the famous Alpujarras rugs *(jarapas)* can still be visited. The village also has a **Visitor Centre** *(Centro de Visitantes)*, which is able to organise a number of varied local excursions. ☎ *958 76 31 27.*

Continue along the A7210. After 2km/1.2mi, take the turn-off to Bubión (3km/1.8mi) and Capileira (4km/2.5mi).

Bubión

Situated at an altitude of 1 296m/4 250ft, the village of Bubión became famous during the revolt of 1569 when its tower was an important centre for *morisco* resistance. As is the case elsewhere in this valley, its houses, with their rugged whitewashed walls and flat rooftops, are reminiscent of the architecture of North Africa.

Capileira

At 1 436m/4 710ft, Capileira is the highest of the three villages in the Poqueira Valley. It has preserved its 16C parish church with an attractive Baroque retable. One of its houses is now home to the **Museo Alpujarreño de Artes y Costumbres Populares**, a museum recreating 19C Alpujarran life through popular arts and customs.

Return to the junction with the A7210.

Mecina Fondales

From here several excursions are possible along the valley formed by the River Trevélez. A minor road leads to the village of Ferreirola, a name which refers to the abundance of iron found throughout this region.

The road continues through an area of outstanding beauty before gradually entering the delightful Trevélez Valley.

ALPUJARRAN HOUSES

The local architecture is perhaps the best example of the region's Moorish past. Those visitors who have set foot in North Africa will be surprised by the strong similarities, with the predominance of south-facing houses searching for the warmth of the sun and often following the relief of this mountainous landscape. The houses are usually built on different levels, forming regularly spaced terraces and steep narrow streets acting as a conduit for rainwater. Traditionally they comprise two floors, the walls of which are completely covered with lime. Their most typical feature is the flat roof, known as a **terrao**, made using large beams of chestnut and battens (*alfarjías*), on top of which a layer of bluish-grey clay known as **launa** is added. Upon contact with water, this layer of clay solidifies to provide a waterproof covering. In the past, these flat roof terraces were used as meeting areas, although nowadays they are predominantly used for storage or for drying clothes, curing food etc.

Pitres

The village is the largest of the seven settlements which make up the *taha* – an old Moorish territorial district comprising Pitres, **Capilerilla**, Mecina, Mecinilla, Fondales, Ferreirola and Atalbéitar.

Pórtugos

Pórtugos is famous for its **Fuente Agria**, a spring of iron-rich water behind the hermitage of Nuestra Señora de las Angustias, at the exit to the village. Tradition says that the water from one of the five pipes has a different taste to that of the others. The best way of testing this theory is to try the water yourself! Opposite, some steps lead to **El Chorreón**, a reddish-coloured waterfall which bears witness to the ferrous qualities of the soil in this area.

Busquístar

This quiet, Mozarabic-style village is the first *pueblo* in the spectacular **Trevélez Valley***. From here the road ascends the left-hand side of the valley to the village which has given its name to the entire valley. However, its dazzlingly white houses are of less interest than its neighbours in the Poqueira Valley.

Trevélez*

Trevélez is formed by three districts, each at a different altitude, and is the highest municipality in Spain (1 600m/ 5 250ft in the *barrio alto*). Behind the village the impressive silhouette of **Mulhacén**, the highest peak on the Iberian Peninsula (3 482m/11 424ft), stands guard.

Beyond Trevélez, the A7210 once more descends the eastern side of the valley. After 6km/4mi, bear right. Once past the abandoned mines of Conjuro, the road links up with the village of Torvizcón and the A 348 running across the southern section of the Alpujarras.

TREVÉLEZ CURED HAM

Ever since **Queen Isabel II** extolled the virtues of its **cured ham** (*jamón*) in the 19C, the name of Trevélez has been synonymous with this gastronomic treat. The secret of its drying sheds (*secaderos*) lies in their special climatic conditions (dry and cold) and the exclusive use of sea salt. White-coloured pigs are bred to produce these large hams (up to 10kg/22lb in weight), which are slightly rounded in shape.

If you wish to continue heading east, follow the A7210 until you reach Juviles.

Juviles

At this point the scenery undergoes a radical change, the verdant nature of the previous two valleys giving way to a wilder landscape. The 16C **Iglesia de Santa María de Gracia** is one of the prettiest churches to be found anywhere in the Granada Alpujarras.

Mecina Bombarón

The landscape here is notably drier, with the appearance of a more Mediterranean-type vegetation, particularly in the **Contraviesa** area to the south, which is famous for its wines. The village, formerly known as Mecina Buenvarón, is dissected by small ravines which act as natural barriers between the different sections of the village. Upon leaving the village, note the Roman bridge over the River Mecina, alongside a more modern construction.

Yegen

This village owes its renown to **Gerald Brenan** – the author of *South from Granada*, a marvellous portrayal of the traditions and customs of the

Alpujarras – who spent seven years here between 1923 and 1934. A plaque marks the house in which he lived during this period.

Válor

Válor is the largest settlement in this part of the Granada Alpujarras. Along with many other churches in this area, the 16C **Iglesia de San José** has been built in Mudéjar style. A late-18C fountain in the square is worthy of particular note. The leader of the *morisco* rebellion in 1568, Don Fernando de Córdoba, known as **Abén Humeya**, was born and lived in Válor.

Laroles

11km/7mi from Válor along the A7208. Laroles stands at the foot of the Puerto de la Ragua (Ragua Pass). Note the unusual tower of its parish church. The hamlets of Picena and Cherín are visible to the south.

Puerto de la Ragua★★

As far as the summit (1 993m/ 6 537ft) the road ascends a gentle slope, along which the landscape gradually acquires a mountainous appearance. Once over the pass, the road narrows and steepens as it descends towards the Guadix Plateau, offering magnificent views of the **Castillo de la Calahorra★★** *(see p 92).*

Capileira

Baza

The origins of this quiet provincial backwater date back to the 4C BC when native Iberians established the settlement of Basti 2km/1.2mi outside the present town. It was here that excavations unearthed the famous **Lady of Baza** (Dama de Baza), a seated sculpture of an Iberian goddess. With the expulsion of the *moriscos* at the end of the 16C, the city entered a period of decline. Nowadays, the only remnants of the former Moorish city are the baths and the maze-like layout of several streets.

Baza is situated in the basin of the same name, 105km/66mi NE of Granada along the A 92 motorway. It lies south of the Negrat Reservoir and close to the northern edge of the attractive Parque Natural de la Sierra de Baza.

🛈 *Plaza Mayor, 2, ☎ 958 86 13 25.*

Colegiata de Santa María de la Encarnación★

This sober, fortress-like collegiate church, built on the site of the former main mosque, is sheltered behind an unusual wall of buttresses. The church has a perfect hall-church ground plan with three aisles of equal height and no transept.

The **plaza Mayor** is fronted by the former town hall, a Renaissance building that now houses the **Museo Municipal**, (☎ 958 86 13 25) which has on display a reproduction of the Dama de Baza, the original of which can be admired in the Museo Arqueológico in Madrid.

Leave the plaza Mayor through the Arco de la Magdalena, an arch on the side of the 18C bell tower, then follow calle Zapatería to the left to what was once the "morisco" quarter of Baza.

The narrow alleyways of this *morisco* district are lined by several buildings of interest: the Mudéjar **Iglesia de San Juan Bautista**; the **Convento de la Merced**, housing the *Virgin of Piety*; and a house with an attractive 17C balcony typical of the period.

Return to the Arco de la Magdalena and head down calle Zapatería. To the left, note the **former abattoirs** *(antiguas carnicerías), dating from 1568. Continue as far as plaza de Santo Domingo.*

The square is dominated by the **Convento de Santo Domingo**, nowadays in a state of poor repair. The better-preserved 17C cloister is concealed on the inside of an early-20C building which once served as a theatre.

Follow calle Dolores. The façade of the 17C-18C **Iglesia de los Dolores** has an unusual Baroque portal framed between two sturdy Solomonic columns.

Continue along calle Dolores, then bear left onto calle del Agua as far as calle Caniles.

Moorish baths*
(Baños árabes)

In calle Caniles, in the Santiago quarter. These simple baths are situated in the old Jewish quarter, next to the Iglesia de Santiago. They date from the Caliphal period (10C) and are some of the oldest to be found anywhere in Europe. The main room is divided by horseshoe arches supported by slender marble columns. The early vaults, through which light entered via star-shaped openings, have not been preserved. The complex is completed by two rectangular rooms which were probably used as a changing room and a caldarium.

B. Kaufmann/MICHELIN

Parque Natural de Sierra de Baza

15km/9.5mi towards Guadix along the A 92. Follow the signposts to the park. From the A 92 junction, continue for a further 5km/3mi to the Visitor Centre in Narváez. ☎ *958 86 10 13.*
Despite its limited infrastructure, this recently created park is able to offer a range of interesting walks for hikers. The Sierra de Baza is surprisingly mountainous, with several peaks above 2 000m/6 560ft. The most common trees found here are oak and pine, including the occasional area of wild pine; typical fauna includes various species of birds of prey.

Plaza Mayor

Costa Tropical

Located to the south of Granada, the Tropical Coast is accessible via the A 44 motorway and the E 902. Motril and Salobreña, the closest towns, are 73km/45mi and 74km/46mi respectively from the provincial capital.

🖪 Palacete de la Najarra, Almuñécar, ☎ 958 63 11 25; Plaza de Goya, Salobreña, ☎ 958 61 03 14.

The Tropical Coast is the name used to describe the 100km/62mi stretch of coastline between La Herradura and La Rábita, characterised by steep descents where mountains swoop down to the sea forming delightful coves. Protected from cold weather systems by the mountain range skirting the coast and tempered by the warm winds from North Africa, this coast has developed into an ideal year-round holiday destination.

Imagen © TURISMO ANDALUZ S.A.

La Herradura

This spectacular bay is situated between **La Punta de la Mona** and **Cerro Gordo**, two watchtowers protecting the **Playa de La Herradura**. Here, as is the case all along the coast in Granada province, the rugged mountains descend to the sea, creating a setting of extraordinary beauty. La Punta de la Mona is home to a pleasure port, the **Puerto Deportivo Marina del Este**.

Almuñécar

The modern name of this coastal town derives from the Arabic *Hins-al-Monacar*, or fortress city, a reference to its strategic position on top of a hill. Its hot climate is the reason for the proliferation of fruits, vegetables and flowers – the other important feature of the local economy – grown under plastic all along this part of the Mediterranean.

Palacete de la Najarra – This small, neo-Moorish palace, built in the second third of the 19C, is now home to the **tourist office** and is an ideal starting point for a visit of Almuñécar. Note the exotic garden inside the palace.

View over the bay at Almuñécar

Castillo de San Miguel* – ☎ 958 63 11 25. This castle of Roman origin bears witness to the succession of occupiers who took up residence here: the Umayyads, Almoravids, Almohads, Nasrids and Christians. It suffered considerable damage in the war against the French in 1808, resulting in the abandonment of the castle until recent times. Under the Nasrids, it served as a palace for the monarchs of the kingdom of Granada. Inside, the dungeon and a single house have survived from this period; the fortified entrance towers were built during the reign of Emperor Charles V. The small museum displays some interesting **models** of the Almuñécar area.

Cueva de los Siete Palacios: Museo Arqueológico – ☎ 958 63 11 25. The town's archaeological museum is housed in a basement of Roman origin. Exhibits include various artefacts unearthed in Phoenician necropolises on the site, the most outstanding of which is the Egyptian **funerary urn*** of Apophis I in grey marble, containing the oldest written document found in Spain.

Parque "El Majuelo" – These small botanical gardens contain a wonderful array of subtropical plants, including 400 species of palm tree. The ruins of an old **Phoenician salting factory** are visible inside the gardens. This particular industry attained such enormous prestige during the period of Greek occupation that figures such as Strabo and Galen refer to **garum**, a special condiment, which was produced here.

Salobreña*

Salobreña is situated by the sea on top of a hill crowned by an imposing **castle**. It is surrounded by fields of sugar cane and orchards and is probably the most attractive of the towns along the stretch of coast within the boundaries of Granada province. Its swathe of whitewashed houses dominates the hillside, the narrow streets awash with colourful bougainvillaea. The town's main attractions are its castle, the **Iglesia de la Virgen del Rosario**, and its splendid beaches, such as the **Playa de El Peñón**.

Castle – *The best view of the castle is from the Almuñécar road.* ☎ 958 61 03 14. Although records show that a castle existed here as early as the 10C, its greatest period of splendour coincided with

A CASTLE OF LEGENDS

Washington Irving wrote that the princesses Zaida, Zoraida and Zorahaida, the daughters of the king of Granada, Mohammed IX, were confined to the sumptuous palace of Salobreña for many years by their father who, following the advice of his astrologers, decided to protect them from everyday temptation, not least that of meeting an undesirable suitor. The three princesses lived here surrounded by luxury, their every need attended to, until their father took them to his palace at the Alhambra. Destiny dictated that they encountered such a temptation on the journey to Granada, when the party fell upon three Christian prisoners who immediately fell in love with the three young the reign of the Nasrids, who transformed it into a luxurious residence which also served as a royal prison.

Access to the interior is via a corner doorway, which leads to the first defensive enclosure. The *alcazaba* (fortress), with its two underground caverns and keep, is at the very heart of the castle.

Motril

Today, this sizeable community of 50 000 inhabitants is the largest town along the Costa Tropical, although this was not always the case. Up until the 18C, when sugar cane was introduced here, resulting in its nickname of "Little Cuba", Motril was nothing more than a small village known only as the residence of the mother of Boabdil, the last king of Granada. Sadly, it has little to offer tourists, who tend to flock to the hotels along the **Playa de Poniente** *(4km/2.5mi SW)*.

From **Motril**, the road runs parallel to the Mediterranean, passing through Torrenueva, **Carchuna**, **Calahonda** and Castell de Ferro. The beaches here are longer and wider than those around Almuñécar. In addition, several medieval watchtowers, such as the Torre de Carchuna, Torrenueva and La Rábita, are visible from the road. From the town of La Rábita, it is worth making the short detour *(5km/3mi)* to **Albuñol**, a *pueblo blanco* nestled in the Sierra de la Contraviesa.

Salobreña

$\mathcal{G}$uadix ★

Guadix is situated at the centre of the depression (hoya) of the same name, 57km/35mi from Granada along the A 92 motorway.

🖪 *Carretera de Granada,* ☎ *958 66 26 65.*

Guadix is a town without borders or a definite perimeter but which is nonetheless perfectly framed by the clay hills around it, and by the heights of the **Sierra Nevada** which act as a magnificent backdrop. This somewhat mysterious *pueblo* conceals many of its secrets in its troglodyte dwellings, which are only partially revealed by the white chimneys which appear everywhere at ground level, silent witnesses of a seemingly endless underground world.

As a staging post between eastern and western Andalucía, this settlement saw a number of different peoples colonise the surrounding area, all of whom have left their mark on modern Guadix. The town reached its peak during the Arab period, from which its fortress *(alcazaba)* survives, although the majority of buildings visible today date from the 17C and 18C.

Plaza de la Constitución

This pretty arcaded square dates from the 16C and 17C; along one of its sides stands the **town hall** *(ayuntamiento)*, built at the beginning of the 17C during the reign of Felipe III.

Cathedral

Work on the cathedral started in 1597 according to designs by **Diego de Siloé**, and continued until 1715, the year in which the impressive Baroque tower was completed. This becomes obvious upon entering the church, where the Gothic architecture of the entrance aisles gives way behind the transept to a Renaissance style which reaches its highest expression in the immense dome adorned with a large lantern covering the false transept. The **Capilla de San Torcuato** *(second chapel to the left of the retrochoir)* was designed by Diego de Siloé and has an entrance arch which is referred to as a "bull's horn", because its width decreases as it curves. The **Fachada de la Encarnación★** *(facing the square)*, is a good example of the theatricality and movement of Baroque architecture. The three horizontal registers of this façade increase in

The name Guadix

Originally known as **Acci** (hence the name *accitanos* given to modern residents of the Guadix), the name of this former Roman camp changed to the more poetic Guadh-Haix, which translates as "the river of life", during the period of Moorish occupation.

View over the town and the church bell-tower

complexity as they converge towards an imaginary point. Behind the cathedral, in calle Santa María, stand the 16C **Palacio Episcopal** (Bishop's Palace), the Hospital de la Caridad and **Palacio de Villalegre** (1592), which has an attractive Renaissance doorway flanked by two solid brick towers.

Barrio de Santiago

This is one of the most typical districts of the town with seigniorial mansions such as the **Palacio de Peñaflor** in which an unusual **balcony** decorated with wood can be seen. The mansion is built around a beautiful Renaissance patio. The seminary *(seminario menor)* next door provides access to the former Arab **alcazaba** (fortress) dating from the 11C. Although the fortress is in poor condition, a tour of it provides the best views of Guadix and the town's troglodyte district.

Back in calle Barradas, flights of steps lead to plazuela de Santiago. At the end of this small square is the **Iglesia de Santiago**, its lovely Plateresque **doorway*** crowned with the shield of Charles V, recognisable by the two-headed eagle and the Golden Fleece. The Mudéjar ceiling inside the church is especially worthy of note.

Calle Ancha, which leads off this square, has a number of fine 19C seigniorial mansions.

Barrio de las Cuevas*

The cave district is situated in the highest part of Guadix, amid a landscape of streams, gullies and small brown hills. The caves are built on different levels, so that those dwellings hollowed into the side of the hills often have their entrance on top of the roof of another cave. Solitary caves can occasionally be seen in an isolated location, occupying a single hillside.

B. Kaufmann/MICHELIN

CAVE DWELLINGS

The special characteristics of the clay soil found in the **Guadix Basin** have made the construction of these unusual dwellings possible. Clay has the property of being easy to work and yet hardening upon contact with air. The end result is a cave which is impermeable, thermally insulated, and which maintains a constant temperature (18°C/64°F) all year round, making it cool during the hot summer months and warm during the cold winters. Guadix alone has around 2 000 inhabited caves, while one of the largest groups of cave dwellings in Europe exists in the surrounding area. The origin of these dwellings is uncertain, although it would appear that most of them were built after the Christian Reconquest and the progressive segregation imposed upon the area's *morisco* population. In Guadix, these inhabitants were gradually expelled from the Santa Ana district and subsequently occupied the cave dwellings in the troglodyte district visible today

Cueva-Museo – *In the Barrio de las Cuevas (follow signposts).* This cave-museum has recreated life in a cave dwelling during the 19C. Several rooms exhibit typical farming and shepherds' tools from the region.

Museo de Alfarería

In the Mozarabic district of San Miguel. This pottery museum is housed in a cave of Moorish origin which has retained some of its historical features, including a well dating from 1650 made from Arab bricks and a large earthenware jar from 1640 buried in the floor and possibly used to store wine. The museum clearly demonstrates the rich tradition of pottery in Granada province, including the famous **accitano pitchers**.

Barrio de Santa Ana

The town's Moorish quarter is a network of narrow alleyways, lined by whitewashed houses decked in flowers and aromatic plants. The **Iglesia de Santa Ana,** built on the site of a mosque in the 15C, can be seen at the heart of the *barrio.* Next to the façade is a Renaissance fountain dating from 1567.

Troglodyte district

*A*round Guadix

Purullena

6km/4mi towards Granada. The **road**** from Guadix crosses a beautiful landscape of tufa rock. Purullena is known for its cave dwellings and its ceramic shops which can be seen on both sides of the road running through the village. The spa of **Cortes y Graena** is reached after 6km/4mi. The road continues to **La Peza** (13km/8mi), passing through an attractive landscape of low-lying clay hills.

La Calahorra*

18.5km/11.5mi SE along the A 92. Hidden behind the peaks of the Sierra Nevada, like an island surrounded by a sea of almond trees, the village of La Calahorra has retained much of its historic past. One of the most spectacular approaches to the village is the route across the Sierra Nevada via the **Puerto de la Ragua**** *(see p 81),* along which the contrast between the Sierra and the Altiplano can be appreciated to the full. This isolated village, crowned by an impressive fortress, stands as proudly now as it did during its time as the capital of the Marquisate of Zenete.

The desolate landscape of the Minas del Marquesado, mines which were abandoned in 1997, is visible 4km/2.5mi from the village.

Castillo de la Calahorra** – ☎ 958 67 70 98. Despite the castle's robust military appearance, a feature en-

Imagen © TURISMO ANDALUZ S.A.

Troglodyte houses in Guadix

B. Morandi/MICHELIN

La Calahorra castle

hanced by the castle's four cylindrical towers, one of Spain's most beautiful **Renaissance patios**** is hidden inside it. The patio was built at the beginning of the 15C in the artistic style of the Italian *quattrocento* and is laid out in a square plan with two sections joined by a splendid **staircase**** comprising three flights of stairs. The decoration, particularly on the doorways and capitals, uses the full range of classical features, including mouldings, candelabra, flowers and storiated columns.

Loja

Loja stands proudly on a hill overlooking the fertile plain of the River **Genil**, halfway between Málaga and Granada. The town is dominated by its fortress, around which developed the old quarter, with its undeniable Moorish air. To the Arabs, it was a place of great strategic importance for their defence of the plain extending east towards Granada. Loja was razed on several occasions during the Reconquest, although it was not until Boabdil handed over the city to the Catholic Monarchs in 1486 that Moorish domination in Loja finally came to end. The year 1800 saw the birth here of **General Narváez**, who controlled Spanish politics in an authoritative manner during the reign of Isabel II.

Loja is located 55km/34mi W of Granada, close to the A 92 motorway and the Iznájar Reservoir.

🛈 *Duque de Valencia, 1, ☎ 958 32 39 49.*

Barrio de la Alcazaba

Loja's historical district *(barrio)* stands on a small promontory, and is characterised by narrow alleyways with evocative names, lined by a number of architectural treasures. Access to the old quarter is either via the Cuesta del Señor hill or by circling the impressively proportioned **Iglesia de la Encarnación**, a church built between the 16C and 18C. Above it stands the **alcazaba**, a fortress which has preserved its keep; the residence of the Christian Governors *(Caserón de los Alcaides Cristianos)*, a house of simple design from the 17C; the Torre Ochavada; and, on the parade ground, the remains of a cistern *(aljibe)*. Calle Moraima leads to the outer limits of the medieval quarter. The view from the Mirador Arqueológico of the **Iglesia de San Gabriel**, a fine 16C Renaissance church, is particularly impressive.

In plaza de Abajo, formerly known as plaza Joaquín Costa, note one of the gates, the 13C **Puerta de Jaufín**, that provided access to the fortress. To the side stands the former granary *(pósito)*, a building that has only retained its lower section.

ANNUNCIATION FAÇADE, IGLESIA DE SAN GABRIEL

The façade of the Iglesia de San Gabriel, attributed to **Diego de Siloé**, is a striking example of 16C Renaissance architecture. The lower section corresponds to the typical design of a triumphal arch, its bay flanked by paired Ionic columns, while the smaller upper tier is crowned by a pediment and flanked by Corinthian columns. In the vaulted niche, a sculptural group featuring the archangel Gabriel and the Virgin Mary represents the Annunciation – hence the name given to the portal of the church.

B. Kaufmann/MICHELIN

Bell-tower of the Iglesia de la Encarnación

Around Loja

Iznájar*

Approximately 30km/19mi NW along the A 92 and A 333.
Iznájar's magnificent **site***, on top of a hill that juts out like a peninsula into the **Iznájar Reservoir** *(embalse)*, offers a foretaste of the charms of this small, delightfully situated Córdoban town close to the border with the province of Granada. Picturesque houses line steep whitewashed streets leading to the upper part of the town, which is dominated by the ochre-coloured stone of the church and the remains of the Moorish castle.

The countryside surrounding Iznájar is never far from view, with several of the town's street corners providing stunning **views**. The panorama from the castle and church quarter takes in far-distant landscapes carpeted in olive groves.

Castle – The origins of the castle date back to the 8C when the Moors built it to take advantage of this stra-

B. Kaufmann/MICHELIN

tegic site, which they named Hisn Ashar. Although it is now in ruins, the remains of sections of wall and several towers are still visible.

Biblioteca Municipal – The municipal library is housed in the former town granary, built during the reign of Carlos III.

Parroquia de Santiago – This 16C Renaissance-style parish church has been built with large pieces of ashlar stone. It is topped by a truncated tower.

Mirador de la Cruz de San Pedro – *At the end of calle Cruz de San Pedro.* This mirador offers **views*** of the fortress and church, the lake and the town.

The lower part of the town is the setting for the **Museo Etnográfico**, an ethnographical museum displaying a collection of implements, ploughing tools and other instruments used to work the land, and the **Casa de las Columnas**, with heraldic decoration on its façade.

Embalse de Iznájar – The 30km/18mi-long Iznájar Reservoir, which is also known as the Lago de Andalucía (Lake of Andalucía), acts as a large dam for the waters of the River Genil. The eastern section of the lake is part of Granada province. The Playa de Valdearenas, on its shoreline, is a popular beach for swimmers and water sports enthusiasts.

The village and dam de Iznájar

Montefrío ★

Montefrío is one of the prettiest towns in the western reaches of Granada province, and enjoys a **setting**★★ that is particularly impressive. Its whitewashed houses with their tiled roofs sit gracefully on two hills which appear like small islands amid a sea of olive groves. Like many of its neighbouring towns and villages, it was highly coveted by both Moors and Christians during the 15C. Several Castilian kings failed in their attempts to conquer Montefrío, before the Catholic Monarchs finally succeeded in taking control of the town in 1486.

The town is nestled amid a landscape of undulating hills, 58km/36mi NW of Granada via the A 329, A 92 and A 335. *It can also be reached from Granada along the N 432 and NO 40.*

🄱 *Plaza de España, 1,* ☎ *958 33 60 04.*

Plaza de España

The town's main square contains three of Montefrío's most important buildings: the impressive bulk of the Iglesia de la Encarnación, the highly recommended **tourist office** and, a little further along, the **town hall** *(ayuntamiento)*, housed in a building dating from the 18C.

Iglesia de la Encarnación

Although this surprising neo-Classical church has been

B. Kaufmann/MICHELIN

attributed to Ventura Rodríguez, there is little proof to substantiate this claim. The church has a circular plan and a half-orange cupola which is visible from all over the town.

Climb up to the Villa section of town along calle del Arco Gracia.

Iglesia de la Villa*

This church was built on top of the hill above the remains of a **Nasrid fortress**, from which several features have been preserved, including the old cistern. The ubiquitous **Diego de Siloé** was responsible for the design of the church, which is a combination of a Gothic structure with Renaissance ornamentation. The single nave, crowned by an elegant pointed vault, is completed by a polygonal chapel with a shell-shaped dome.

Walk down to plaza de España and follow calle Enrique Amat to placeta del Pósito.

Placeta del Pósito

The town's 18C former **granary** *(pósito)*, a building of simple design, dominates this small square.

From here, head up Monte del Calvario to the Iglesia de San Antonio.

Iglesia de San Antonio

The church was originally part of the Franciscan Convento de San Antonio, which ceased its religious function and became a flour factory known as "La Máquina" following the confiscation of church property during the 19C. The Iglesia de San Antonio de Padua is Baroque in style with a handsome west façade in the form of a three-sectioned retable, the upper part of which contains a statue of St Anthony in a niche. From here, it is well worth walking along calle Cruz del Calvario for one of the best **views**★★ of the town.

Nice view of Montefrío

Tower and dome of the Iglesia de la Encarnación, Montefrío

*A*round Montefrío

Peña de los Gitanos*

Approximately 5km/3mi from Montefrío along the Illora road. After passing the Mesón Curro to your right, continue as far as a road signposted to Peña de los Gitanos. As this is a private road and property, leave your car at the beginning of the dirt track and continue on foot (15min).

The track climbs gently through olive groves to a fork. Take the path to the right; after passing an abandoned mine, a first area of meadow comes into view. Cross the meadow, passing a dolmen to the right, to reach a second meadow dotted with oak trees. The best-preserved megalithic tombs are located here. Several are dotted around the meadow, although the most spectacular is to the right, behind a small group of oak trees. This particular **dolmen*** has a corridor and burial chamber with a perfectly preserved roof.

Moclín

33.5km/21mi E. Head towards Illora, then follow the NO 19 as far as the N 432. Bear left towards Alcalá la Real until you reach Puerto López. The road passes through the town of **Illora**, dominated by the silhouette of the enormous 16C Iglesia de la Encarnación. The road then climbs slightly, skirting narrow bends until the impressive sight of the **Castillo de la Mota*** suddenly appears on top of a hill, dominating the small town of Moclín. This double-enclosure fortress, dating from the Nasrid period, is accessed via an angled doorway. Several buildings stand inside the fortress confines: the former 16C granary *(pósito)*, the Iglesia de la Encarnación, from the same century, and, higher up, the remains of the keep and a cistern.

Priego de Córdoba★★

78km/49mi NW of Granada along the N 432 and A 340, and 24km/15mi W of Alcalá la Real. This Córdoban town is situated in an area of outstanding beauty close to the northwestern boundaries of the province of Granada.
🛈 *Calle del Río, 33,* ☎ *957 70 06 25.*

The delightful town of Priego de Córdoba, nestled at the foot of the Pico de la Tiñosa (1 570m/5 150ft), is considered to be the capital of Cordoban Baroque, as borne out by the numerous buildings erected during this sumptuous period in the town's history. Priego reached its economic zenith in the 18C thanks to the silk industry, which was to generate untold artistic and cultural splendour.

Follow signs to the town centre (centro ciudad) and park near plaza de la Constitución, which is fronted by the town hall (ayuntamiento).

Hospital-Iglesia de San Juan de Dios

In plaza de la Constitución, to the right of the town hall. The hospital was founded in 1637 by Juan de Herrera and completed in 1717. The first feature of interest inside the building is the attractive cloistered patio. The handsome Baroque church, with its single nave and fine echini-adorned cupola above the transept, stands to the rear, on the right-hand side. Several broken cornices run along the upper sections of the side walls, providing the church with a certain dynamism. The building is completely whitewashed, with vegetal decoration arranged in bands or garlands. The Virgin of Mercy (Virgen de las Mercedes) presides over the main altarpiece, which is also Baroque.

Exit calle Ribera and head along paseo del Abad Palomino.

Castle

The significant remains of this sober and imposing fortress, of Moorish origin but modi-

Iglesia de la Asunción

fied in the 13C and 14C, can be seen from the **paseo del Abad Palomino**. The wall is punctuated with square towers, including the **keep**, with its paired windows. It is possible to walk around most of the outside of the castle, where houses can be seen built against the wall.

Parroquia de la Asunción*

This 16C late-Gothic church was remodelled in the 18C in Baroque style. Note also the fine Renaissance portal on the right-hand side. The bright, spacious interior comprises three aisles crowned with arris vaults and decorated keystones, and an echini-adorned cupola above pendentives. The presbytery is dominated by an impressive carved and painted 16C Mannerist-style **retable**. In the chapels, several altarpieces and a Christ attributed to Alonso de Mena are also worthy of note.

El Sagrario★★ – This chapel, which opens onto the Evangelist nave, is a masterpiece of Priego and Spanish Baroque. Its ground plan consists of a rectangular antechamber leading into an octagonal space surrounded by an ambulatory, in the centre of which stands the chapel. Light plays an important part in the overall scene, and is intensified by the whiteness of the walls and ceiling, inundating the central area with a dazzling brightness and creating a magical atmosphere. The interior is enhanced by the sublime **plasterwork**★★★ by the local artist Francisco Javier Pedrajas (1736-1817), which covers the entire chapel. Pay particular attention to the keystone of the large cupola which is adorned with numerous small heads. Lower down, a sculpture of an Apostle can be seen against each pillar. The decoration combines plant motifs, rocaille work and scenes with characters illustrating themes found in both the Old and New Testaments. Despite the profuse decoration, the overall effect is one of lightness and delicacy, and is without doubt one of the highlights of a visit to Priego de Córdoba.

Barrio de la Villa★★

Tucked away behind the church, this charming quarter dating back to medieval and Moorish times is characterised by narrow, winding streets and flower-decked whitewashed houses. The combination of myriad colours and scents has made the Barrio de la Villa one of Andalucía's archetypal sights. A leisurely stroll along calle Jazmines, calle Bajondillo, calle Reales and through plaza de San Antonio is particularly recommended.

El Adarve★

To the north of the Barrio de la Villa, this delightful balcony looks onto the Subbética mountain range. The impressive **views**, attractive lamp posts, iron benches and contemplative atmosphere transport visitors back to bygone days.

Return to the starting point of paseo del Abad Palomino and follow carrera Álvarez.

THE BROTHERS OF THE AURORA

The brotherhood of the Iglesia de la Aurora keeps alive a time-honoured tradition every Saturday night, when it takes to the streets of Priego de Córdoba singing songs in honour of the Virgin.

Iglesia de la Aurora

The former 15C church was remodelled in the 18C by Juan de Dios Santaella in Baroque style, although it has preserved its 16C tower and belfry. It has a fine polychrome marble Baroque portal on two levels, presided over by the Virgin of the Aurora between two Solomonic columns. The single-nave interior has profuse Baroque decoration.

Retrace your steps as far as plaza de San Pedro.

Iglesia de San Pedro

The Baroque additions to this church were completed in 1690. The interior contains some interesting statuary, including an outstanding **Immaculate Conception*** in the *camarín* behind the main altarpiece; this statue is attributed by some to Diego de Mora, and by others to Alonso Cano. The first chapel to the side of the Evangelist nave houses an image of the **Virgin of Solitude**, while the last chapel on the Epistle nave contains a delightful wooden **recumbent Christ** (1594) attributed to Pablo de Rojas, on display inside a glass urn.

Head along calle Pedrajas.

Carnicerías Reales

The former royal abattoir and market was built in the 16C along Classical lines, and is a somewhat surprising addition to a town dominated by Baroque architecture. The simple stone doorway, presided over by the coat of arms of the Fernández de Córdoba family, is adorned with two unusual engaged columns. The square-shaped interior has a central patio and towers on its corners. To the rear, to the right of the window with views of the local countryside, a spiral staircase descends to the room where animals were slaughtered. Nowadays it is used as an exhibition hall.

Return to plaza de la Constitución, at the start of calle del Río.

Iglesia de las Angustias

If closed, knock on the door of the adjacent building; the nuns from the school will show visitors around. The church was built in 1772 by Juan de Dios Santaella. Its outstanding feature is the twin-sectioned polychrome doorway with its abundant broken lines. Note also the unusual Virgin and Child in the vaulted niche and the finely worked *estípites* on the lower section. The church belfry can be seen to the left side.

The inside of the church, which is surprisingly small in size, is Rococo. The area above the altar is covered by an attractive moulded dome above pendentives. On the gilded retable, the middle sculptural group, depicting the Virgin with the dead

Christ in her arms, stands out; this work is from the Granada School and dates from the late 18C. Also worthy of note are two terracotta sculptures by José Risueño beneath this work.

Follow **calle del Río**, which is lined by several seigniorial houses. The **birthplace of Niceto Alcalá-Zamora** (1877-1949), President of the Second Republic, is now home to the town's tourist office.

Iglesia del Carmen

This church was built in the 18C in the transitional style between Baroque and neo-Classical. The façade combines elements of both styles and has a tower directly incorporated onto it. The portal, the last feature to be built, is pure neo-Classical.

Fuentes del Rey y de la Salud**

At the end of calle del Río. These two fountains, known as the Fountains of the King *(Rey)* and Health *(Salud)*, form the most well-known sight in Priego de Córdoba.

The older of the two, the **Fuente de la Salud***, was sculpted in the 16C by Francisco del Castillo. It is a stone frontispiece built in Mannerist style with, at its centre, a small niche containing the Virgin of Health, hence its name. The

green of the vegetation contrasts with the golden stone, helping to create a charming scene enhanced by the proximity of the lavish **Fuente del Rey**★★, which was completed at the beginning of the 19C. Both its dimensions and the richness of its design, characterised by curves and counter-curves, evoke the gardens of a Baroque palace. It is arranged on three levels with 139 jets spouting water from the mouths of the same number of masks. The sculptural groups are the work of Remigio del Mármol: the central work represents Neptune's chariot and Amphitrite. The lion fighting the snake on the top section is attributed to the neo-Classical sculptor J Alvarez Cubero.

Head along calle Obispo Pérez Muñoz as far as carrera de las Monjas.

Museo Histórico Municipal

This local museum, housed in the birthplace of the painter and illustrator Adolfo Lozano Sidro (1872-1935), displays a number of archaeological exhibits discovered in and around Priego de Córdoba.

Other Baroque churches of interest include the **Iglesia de las Mercedes** and the **Iglesia de San Francisco**, the latter fronted by a neo-Classical portal.

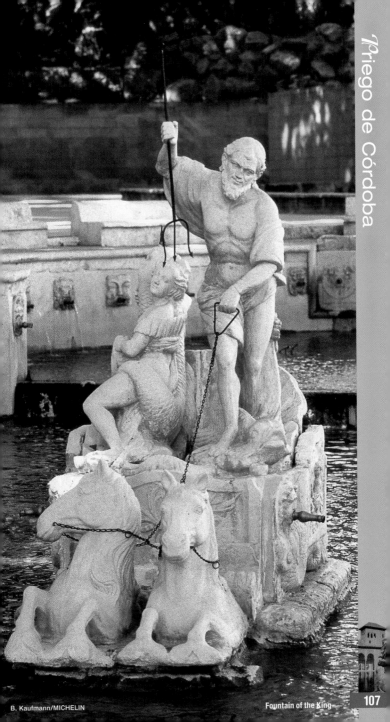

B. Kaufmann/MICHELIN

Fountain of the King

$\mathcal{S}$ierra Nevada★★

The Sierra Nevada mountain range is situated southeast of the city of Granada.

The fastest and quickest route from Granada is along the A 395. In Pradollano (38km/ 24mi) visitors will have to leave their vehicles in the underground car park. A more attractive alternative is to combine the two itineraries suggested below.

By bus: the BONAL company operates several daily services from Granada to Pradollano, leaving from the bus stop next to the Palacio de Congresos – ☎ 958 27 31 00.

It comes as something of a surprise to many visitors to find a mountain range of such magnitude at such a southerly latitude. Standing proudly above the city of Granada, this impressive sierra is the second-highest range in Europe after the Alps, with its highest peaks perpetually capped with snow. The Sierra Nevada's many attractions include a superb ski resort and magnificent high-mountain landscapes characterised by steep-sided valleys and breathtaking ravines.

This monumental mountain range stretches across a distance of over 90km/56mi, occupying a total area in excess of 170 000ha/420 070 acres (86 208ha/213 020 acres of which are part of the **national park**). Snow and ice, both of which are present for much of the year, have eroded this young mountain chain during the course of time to create a sculpted, twisted profile. Fourteen of the Sierra Nevada's peaks are over 3 000m/9 840ft high, culminating in the three highest summits of **Mulhacén** (3 482m/11 424ft), **Veleta** (3 394m/11 132ft) and **Alcazaba** (3 371m/11 057ft), all of which lie in the western part of the range.

When to visit?

Any time of year is a good time to visit the Sierra Nevada. Its ski resort offers a range of options to visitors, including downhill skiing, various excursions, and a number of treks to some of the highest snow-capped peaks. In summer, hiking and horse riding are popular activities. Snow can start to fall in October and in some years it has even been known to snow in June; despite this, the Sierra Nevada is renowned for its glorious sunny days for two-thirds of the year, when the combination of sun, the whiteness of the snow and the blue sky create a scene of almost unparalleled beauty.

Information Centres

Centro de Visitantes del Dornajo – At Km 23 on the Sierra Nevada road – ☎ 958 34 06 25. The El Dornajo visitor centre is an ideal starting-point for a visit to the Sierra Nevada, with its wide range of information on the park (models, exhibitions etc), an excellent bookshop and the introduction it provides to

THE "ICE VENDORS"

The name *neveros* was given to those men who supplied ice to the city of Granada in bygone days. These fearless souls would climb up to the snow-capped peaks of the Sierra Nevada in groups of around ten men and with the help of mules and donkeys would load up and transport ice to the hospitals, shops and bars in the city. They worked from dusk onwards, taking advantage of the cool of the night to return to Granada without losing any of their precious cargo due to the heat. This activity was so important that even in the 18C operating licences existed and regulations governing it were already in place. The trade in ice collapsed around 1920 with the establishment of the first ice factories.

the region's gastronomy and arts and crafts. The centre also organises a range of activities for visitors, including high-mountain hikes, excursions and bicycle hire.

Punto de Información del Parque Nacional de Sierra Nevada – *In Pampaneira (plaza de la Libertad)* – ☎ *958 76 31 27.* This centre organises activities and tours in the Sierra Nevada and Alpujarras.

Punto de Información del Puerto de la Ragua – *At Km 1 on the Puerto de la Ragua road* – ☎ *958 34 55 28; www.laragua.net*

Hiking routes

Hiking possibilities in the Sierra Nevada are almost endless. Visitors are advised

Imagen © TURISMO ANDALUZ S.A.

The Alhambra and the Sierra Nevada

to head for the visitor centre before setting out, to obtain information on the marked walks available and the length of time needed. The most popular departure points are the following: the village of Güejar-Sierra, the El Dornajo visitor centre and the **Albergue Universitario** (University Hostal). The most interesting routes are the climb to the **Laguna de las Yeguas** lagoon and the ascents of **Pico Veleta** and **Mulhacén**.

Sierra Nevada ski resort✳✳

The resort was built in 1964 and held its first major sporting event, a **World Cup** downhill, in 1977. However, just two years later, the company responsible for the management of the resort was forced to consider closure due to its lack of profitability. The situation improved during the 1980s, a period which coincided with various proposals relating to the protection of the Sierra Nevada. In the 1990s the resort was chosen to host the **1995 World Skiing Championships**; however, due to a lack of snow these were postponed until the following year. The investments made for this event have transformed the resort into one of the best in Spain, with a ski area of around 60km/37.5mi, 45 runs and 20 lifts. Other options on offer here include evening ski-

Imagen © TURISMO ANDALUZ S.A.

Ski resort in the Sierra Nevada

ing at weekends. The resort also has a full range of apartment and hotel accommodation in **Pradollano**.

Driving tours

Construction of the first road in the Sierra Nevada began in 1914. By 1923 it had reached Pinos Genil and in 1935 the section to the Pico Veleta was officially opened. Since then, this road has been used for access to the highest peaks within the range. However, the recent designation of the Sierra Nevada as a **Natural Park** in 1989 and then a **National Park** in 1999 has resulted in severe restrictions on the use of these roads. Two control posts, one on the northern section (Borreguiles crossroads), the other to the south (Hoya del Portillo), limit access within the park for private vehicles. The two itineraries suggested below take into account these restrictions. *Visitors are, however, advised to check road conditions prior to departure.*
From Granada to El Dornajo** – *Only possible in summer. Approximately 1hr.*

Leave Granada on the old mountain road *(carretera de la Sierra)*. After 8km/5mi turn off towards Pinos Genil. The road passes through an attractive landscape, skirting the Canales Reservoir *(embalse)* before reaching **Güejar-Sierra**. Head out of the village in the direction of Maitena. After crossing the Genil, the road follows the course of the river, climbing along sharp, steep bends to the Hotel del Duque, now a seminary, before arriving at the El Dornajo visitor centre.
From El Dornajo to the Borreguiles crossroads** – From the El Dornajo Visitor Centre follow the road to the left which climbs up to the Collado de las Sabinas mountain pass, an ascent which is both steep and punctuated with sharp bends. The scenery here is one of native pines, with fine views of the Genil Valley from the road. Once past the Collado de las Sabinas pass, the road continues to Pradollano. From here it is possible to reach the Borreguiles crossroads.

MULHACÉN

According to legend, the name of the highest peak on mainland Spain originates from a story which recounts that the king of Granada, Muley-Hacén, the father of Boabdil, is buried here. The king fell in love with a beautiful Christian maiden by the name of Zoraida, who, after the king's death in Mondújar Castle, had him buried on the highest peak of the Sierra Nevada to hide him from his enemies.

Valle del Lecrín ★

Head south from Granda along the N 323, then turn off the main road in Dúrcal.

The little-known Lecrín Valley is a delight for visitors. The road winds its way through orange groves, passing small villages sitting on the slopes of the valley along the way.

Dúrcal

This village of Moorish origin has a charming main square, the **plaza de España**.

Nigüelas

Nigüelas is one of the prettiest settlements in the valley. The town hall *(ayuntamiento)* is installed in the 16C Palacio de los Zayas. The town's most interesting building is the 14C **Las Laerillas oil mill**★ *(ask for the keys at the town hall)*, inside which the presses, measuring instruments, olive bins and, in particular, two **large mills**, can still be seen. One of these mills is known as the *molino de sangre* (blood mill), so called because it was powered by an animal; the other mill was hydraulically operated.

Mondújar

The Mudéjar-style church in Mondújar is crowned by an impressive tower. The neighbouring village of Lecrín, a word of Arabic origin meaning "happiness", has given its name to the valley. The road continues along the Torrente river valley, skirting the villages of Murchas, Restábal, **Melegís** and **Saleres.** The churches in Melegís and Saleres have managed to preserve some Mudéjar *azulejos* on their towers.

R. Mattes/MICHELIN

A FAMILIAR SIGHT IN THE ANDALUSIAN COUNTRYSIDE

For the past three decades and more the lofty silhouette of this impressive metal bull has graced the tops of Spanish hillsides, establishing itself as one of the most characteristic features of the country's road network. Originally erected in 1956 as part of an advertising campaign for the Osborne sherry and brandy company, they were on the point of disappearing from the Spanish landscape altogether in 1988, following the introduction of a law banning advertising along roads outside of urban areas. Although the company subsequently removed its name, leaving just the bulls in place, the controversy remained. Legal moves to have the bulls removed sparked a debate that received widespread media coverage, resulting in the signing of petitions and the formation of associations to preserve them. Their defenders were of the opinion that these black bulls had gone beyond their original marketing purpose and had become a decorative feature which was now an integral part of the Spanish landscape and a symbol of the country. As a result of this campaign, the regional parliament (Junta de Andalucía) classified the bulls as official historical monuments, thus enabling the bulls to live to fight another day!

H. Champollion/MICHELIN

Directory

Transports

DIRECTORY

Airport – 15km/9mi W along the A 92 motorway, ☎ 958 24 52 00. A bus service operates between the city centre and airport, departing from the Palacio de Congresos, ☎ 958 27 86 77 or 958 13 13 09.

Trains – The railway station is on avenida de Andalucía, ☎ 958 27 12 72. Regular services operate to most towns in Granada province and the majority of major Spanish cities.

RENFE (Spanish State Railways) office: calle Reyes Católicos, 63, ☎ 902 24 02 02.

City buses – Buses serve all parts of the city, including the major monuments and suburbs. A one-way ticket costs €0.90, a 9-trip ticket €5, and a 20-trip ticket €10 (☎ 900 710 900).

Bus station – *Carretera de Jaén*, ☎ 958 18 54 80.

Buses operate from here to every provincial capital within Andalucía, the majority of major Spanish cities and several European capitals.

A daily bus service from Granada to the Sierra Nevada is operated by Bonal, ☎ 958 27 31 00.

Taxis – ☎ 958 28 06 54, 958 15 14 61

Horse-drawn carriages – These can be hired near the Puerta Real for tours of Granada's main tourist sites.

Sightseeing

Bonoturístico – This general ticket covers entrance to the Alhambra, Generalife, cathedral, Capilla Real, La Cartuja, Monasterio de San Jerónimo and the Parque de las Ciencias. It also includes nine journeys on the city's bus network and a 24-hour ticket on the *bus turístico*.

The ticket can be purchased from the Alhambra and Capilla Real ticket offices, as well as from two branches of the Caja de Ahorros de Granada savings bank *(60, plaza de Isabel la Católica; and in the Neptuno shopping centre)*. When you buy the ticket, you will need to specify the time and date of your visit to the Alhambra.

Cost: €18, or €20 if purchased in advance from Caja de Ahorros de Granada branches (valid for 7 days).

For information and reservations, contact the Caja General de Ahorros de Granada, ☎ 902 100 095 (open Mon-Fri, 8.30am-9pm; Sat, 9am-2pm).

Legado Andalusí (The Legacy of al-Andalus foundation) – For information on cultural itineraries and routes, ☎ 958 22 59 95, www.legadoandalusi.es

Where to Eat

The restaurants listed in this section have been chosen for their surroundings, ambience, typical dishes or unusual character. Prices specified correspond to the average cost of both an inexpensive and expensive meal and are given as a guideline only. Restaurants are classified into three categories based on price:

- 🍽 Budget: under €15 (See Tapas)
- 🍽🍽 Moderate: between €15 and €30
- 🍽🍽🍽 Expensive: over €30

🍽🍽 **Chikito** – *Plaza del Campillo, 9 – ☎ 958 22 33 64 – Reservation recommended – €20/25– Closed Wed.* A hugely popular restaurant and bar frequented by artists and intellectuals such as García Lorca in the 1930s. The Chikito is renowned for serving local specialities and superb cured hams.

🍽🍽 **Mariquilla** – *Lope de Vega, 2 – ☎ 958 52 16 32 – 🖼 – €22/29 – Closed Sun evening, Mon and 15 Jul-31 Aug.* Do not be deceived by appearances: although its decor may not be anything special, the Mariquilla is one of the best restaurants in Granada and is excellent value for money.

🍽🍽 **Mirador de Morayma** – *Pianista Gracia Carrillo, 2 – ☎ 958 22 82 90 – €24/30– Closed Sun in Jul-Aug and Sun eve the rest of the year.* With its plant-filled terrace, dining rooms with views of the Alhambra and welcoming, rustic-style decor, this restaurant is one of the most romantic in the city. The menu includes local specialities such as broad beans with ham *(habas con jamón)* and lamb chops *(chuletas de cordero).*

Gastronómico

☺☻ **La Ermita en la Plaza de Toros** – *Avenida Doctor Olóriz, 25 (at the bullring)* – ☎ *958 29 02 57* – ▤ – *€26/35*. Its unusual location within the confines of the city's bullring and its tasteful decoration of exposed brickwork, wooden tables, rustic-style chairs and bullfighting memorabilia on the walls have made this a popular restaurant in which to enjoy typical Andalusian cuisine. The restaurant is on the first floor, and there is a **tapas bar** on the ground floor.

☺☻☻ **Ruta del Veleta** – *In Cenes de la Vega* – *Carretera de Sierra Nevada, 136 – 8km/5mi from Granada* – ☎ *958 48 61 34* – *€40*. An elegant and very popular restaurant, whose decor includes dozens of ceramic jugs hanging from the ceiling. During the winter, the owners also open a restaurant they own in the Sierra Nevada.

In Alcalá la Real

☺☻ **El Curro** – *Ramón y Cajal, 6* – ☎ *953 58 30 50* – *€15/18* – *Closed Wed.* This restaurant is first and foremost a bar popular with locals. Although there is a somewhat nondescript dining room, regulars tend to eat in a more attractive room with a low ceiling and fireplace. Specialities here include grilled meats and ham.

along the Costa Tropical

☺☻ **Vizcaya** – *Paseo de las Flores (Playa de San Cristóbal)* – *Almuñécar* – ☎ *958 63 57 12* – *€9/30* – *Closed Nov.* This pleasant restaurant alongside an attractive pebble beach serves a choice of paellas, grilled meats and fish from the Biscay region, from which it takes its name. A lively atmosphere during the day, transforming into a more romantic ambience in the evening.

☺☻ **Antonio** – *Bajos del Paseo, 12 – Almuñécar* – ☎ *958 63 00 20* – *€26/35*. A restaurant with a solid reputation specialising in fish and seafood for the past 30 years. In the words of its owner: "We never use frozen products, only the freshest ingredients." The lobster, swordfish and Jabugo cured ham are particularly recommended.

In Loja

The nearby village of **Riofrío** has had an excellent reputation for its trout since the 17C. For dessert, why not try another local speciality, the cakes known as **roscos de Loja**.

In Montefrío

☺ **Mesón Coronichi** – *Avenida La Paz, 32* – ☎ *958 33 61 46* – *€12/18*. A good restaurant in which to sample the tasty local cuisine, including its speciality, *relleno de carnaval*, a type of meatball.

In Priego de Córdoba

☺☻ **La Fuente de Zagrilla** – *In the upper part of Zagrilla, approximately 100m/110yd from the Villa Turística* – ☎ *957 70 37 34* – *€15/20* – *Closed Mon in winter.* The simple yet excellent cuisine at this restaurant with a small terrace and patio includes hearty vegetable soups, meat dishes and pineapple flan.

apas

It is rare for tapas bars to list prices. Tapas or the larger *raciones* can vary enormously from one bar to the next, although as a general rule the standard is generally good, with prices rarely exceeding €15 per person for an informal meal.

Bodegas Castañeda – *Almireceros, 1–3* – ☎ *958 21 54 64*. The bar and tables in this typical *bodega*, its decor enhanced by the myriad bottles on display, are often full with customers enjoying the delicious tapas, hams and cheeses served here. A good central location just a few metres from plaza Nueva.

Casa Enrique – *Acera del Darro, 8* – ☎ *958 25 50 08* – *Closed Sun*. The Casa Enrique is run by a friendly owner who is justifiably proud of his large wine cellar. The bar, nestled between a bank and a jewellery store in one of the city's busiest shopping streets, serves delicious cured hams and excellent wines that can be enjoyed by the glass.

Los Diamantes – *Navas, 28* – *Closed Sun and Mon*. This bar, in a pedestrianised street lined with bars and restaurants, specialises in excellent-quality fish and seafood.

La Trastienda – *Placeta de Cuchilleros, 11*. Founded in 1836. Once through the small entrance door, descend a couple of steps to get to a traditional grocery store with tapas counter. The excellent *chorizo* is highly recommended, either standing at the bar, or sitting down in the pleasant room to the rear.

Pilar del Toro – *Hospital de Santa Ana, 12* – ☎ *958 22 38 47*. Housed in an old house dating from 1789, the Pilar del Toro is worth a visit for its distinctive architecture alone. The iron gate leads to the bar with a small counter to the left and a large Andalusian patio to the right, and an attractive restaurant on the first floor.

Imagen © TURISMO ANDALUZ S.A.

Gazpacho

))))here to Stay

Hotels listed below are divided into three categories based on the price of a single room, excluding VAT (7%), and have been chosen for their location, comfort, good value-for-money, and in some cases, their particular charm. The two prices listed under each hotel represent the cost of a single room in low season and a double room in high season.

- ⊖ Budget: under €50
- ⊖⊜ Moderate: between €50 and €80
- ⊖⊜⊜ Expensive: over €80

⊖ **Los Jerónimos** – *Gran Capitán, 1 –* ☎ *958 29 44 61– Fax 958 25 45 00 –* ▤ *– 41 rooms – €39/59.* A well-appointed hotel with modern rooms. Room 502 has a terrace with views of the Alhambra and part of the city. Good value for money.

⊖⊜ **Los Tilos** – *Plaza Bib-Rambla, 4 –* ☎ *958 26 67 12 – Fax 958 26 68 01 –* ▤ *– 30 rooms – €36/65 (including VAT) –* ☐ *€5.* This no-frills hotel fronts a charming square filled with flower stalls, just a few metres from the cathedral. Although on the basic side, the rooms are comfortable, some with the bonus of a view over the plaza.

⊖⊜ **Maciá Plaza** – *Plaza Nueva, 4 –* ☎ *958 22 75 36 – Fax 958 22 75 33 –* ▤ *– 44 rooms – €47.80/70 –* ☐ *€5.50.* A recently renovated hotel occupying a four-storey building with an attractive façade in a central square at the foot of the Alhambra. Standard-quality rooms with carpets and wicker furniture.

⊖⊜ **América** – *Real de la Alhambra, 53 –* ☎ *958 22 74 71 – Fax 958 22 74 70 –* ▤ *– 16 rooms, 1 suite – €68.50/107 –* ☐ *€7 – Restaurant €16 – Closed Nov-Mar.* A small, family-run hotel in a 19C house superbly located within the confines of the Alhambra. A warm welcome and friendly service are the trademarks of the América, which also has a pleasant patio.

⊖⊜⊜ **Carmen de Santa Inés** – *Placeta de Porras, 7 –* ☎ *958 22 63 80 – Fax 958 22 44 04 –* ▤ *– 9 rooms – €80/105 –* ☐ *€10.* Elegant rooms and impressive views of the Alhambra are the highlights of this charming hotel in a typical villa in the Albaicín. On fine days, breakfast can be enjoyed under a pergola overlooking the city's most famous attraction.

⊖⊜⊜ **Palacio de Santa Inés** – *Cuesta de Santa Inés, 9 –* ☎ *958 22 23 62 – Fax 958 22 24 65 –* ▤ *– 13 rooms – from €100 –* ☐ *€8.* This 16C Mudéjar-inspired building is situated in the Albaicín district, with several rooms enjoying views of Granada's number one attraction. In the charming colonnaded patio, you can still make out what's left of the building's original Renaissance frescoes.

⊖⊜⊜ **Parador de Granada** – *Alhambra –* ☎ *958 22 14 40 –* ▤ *– 34 rooms, 2 suites – €245 –* ☐ *€13.* This superb parador at the heart of the Alhambra was originally the 15C Convento de San Francisco, founded by the Catholic Monarchs. Magnificent views of the Generalife gardens and the Sierra Nevada. Even if you don't get to stay here, try and find time to have a drink on the hotel terrace overlooking the Generalife gardens.

In Alcalá la Real

⊖ **Río de Oro** – *Alamos, 4 –* ☎ *953 58 03 37 –* ▤ *– 9 rooms – €18/35.* This centrally located, family-run hotel offers well-appointed rooms, some of which have a balcony overlooking a square and park. Good value for money.

☞ **Torrepalma** – *Conde de Torrepalma, 2 –* ☎ *953 58 18 00 – Fax 953 58 17 12 – 38 rooms –* €*45/60 –* ☕ €*4.50.* The only slight inconvenience is its location along one of Alcalá's busiest and noisiest shopping streets.

In Alhama de Granada

☞ **El Ventorro** – *3km/1.8mi from Alhama de Granada towards Jatar on the GR 141 –* ☎*/Fax 958 35 04 38 – 19 rooms –* €*25/45 (including breakfast).* This hotel on the banks of the Alhama River has small, sober rooms which have nonetheless been tastefully decorated. The restaurant serves simple but tasty cuisine.

☞☗ **Balneario** – *Carretera de Granada – 3km/1.8mi N of Alhama de Granada –* ☎ *958 35 00 11 – Fax 958 35 02 97 – 116 rooms –* €*54/90 –* ☕ €*5.32 – Open Mar-Nov.* The origins of these springs date back to Roman times, although they acquired great renown during the Caliphal period. The present building was built in the 19C. The most spectacular feature is the *aljibe*, a delightful **Moorish cistern**[*] into which the spring's thermal waters gush at a temperature of 47°C/116°F. It is contained within a room built over a Roman basement with an octagonal vault supported by 11C Caliphal arches. The owners have a second hotel, the **Baño Nuevo**, nearby. The clientele here tends to be elderly.

In the Alpujarras

☞ **España** – *Avenida de la Alpujarra, 42 – Lanjarón –* ☎ *958 77 01 87 – Fax 958 77 01 78 – 36 rooms –* €*34/52.50 (including breakfast and VAT).* This early-20C hotel in the centre of Lanjarón has been frequented in the past by illustrious guests such as García Lorca and Manolete. All the rooms have extremely high ceilings.

☞ **Alcazaba de Busquístar** – *On the GR 421 in Busquístar, 4km/2.5mi from Trevélez towards Juviles –* ☎ *958 85 86 87 – Fax 958 85 86 93 – 43 rooms –* €*39/65 –* ☕ €*4 – Restaurant* €*12.* A hotel which has used typical local materials in its construction, including stone slabs, baked clay floors and whitewashed walls. The rooms are spacious and have terraces with superb views over the sierra.

☞ **Alquería de Morayma** – *Along the A 348, 3km/1.8mi from Cádiar towards Torvizcónctra –* ☎*/Fax 958 34 32 21 –* 🖵 *– 13 rooms, 5 apartments –* €*48/59 –* ☕ €*3.* A small country hotel with views of the mountains and the village of Cádiar. Facilities include a bar, restaurant, and a *bodega* decorated with earthenware casks. Good value for money.

☞☗ **Villa Turística de Bubión** – *Barrio Alto – Bubión –* ☎ *958 76 39 09 – Fax 958 76 39 05 – 43 apartments –* €*55/79 –* ☕ €*6.28 – Restaurant* €*12.60.* Simple, traditional-style apartments with kitchen, lounge, bathroom and bedroom. The restaurant is one of the best in the area with specialities such as kid, trout and locally made sausages.

Along the Costa Tropical

☞☗ **Casablanca** – *Plaza San Cristóbal, 4 – Almuñécar –* ☎ *958 63 55 75 – Fax 958 63 55 89 – 35 rooms –* 🖵 **P** *–* €*45/65 –* ☕ €*3.* With its raspberry-coloured façade and impressive dome, the hotel's architectural emphasis is resolutely Moroccan, enhanced by tasteful marble features and crystal chandeliers in the bedrooms. Advance booking recommended.

Salobreña – *At Km 323 along the Málaga–Almería road, 3km/1.8mi from Salobreña towards Málaga –* ☎ *958 61 02 61 – Fax 958 61 01 01 – 195 rooms –* 🖵 **P** *–* €*36/75 (including breakfast).* This large tourist complex, with its gardens and swimming pool, comprises several modern buildings with rooms overlooking the sea, known here as the Costa Rocosa (Rocky Coast). The views of the Mediterranean are superb and the complex is built away from the road so that the only sound here is of the waves breaking on the shore.

In Guadix

🍴 **Comercio** – *Mira de Amezcua, 3* – ☎ *958 66 05 00* – *Fax 958 66 50 72* – 🖵 – *40 rooms, 2 suites* – *€40/60* – 🍽 *€6*. This attractive hotel dating from the beginning of the 20C offers guests spacious rooms and a good restaurant. Specialities here include lamb with honey *(cordero a la miel)*, Guadix soup and the delicious custard pudding known as *tocino de cielo* (literally "bacon from heaven").

🍴 **Cuevas Pedro Antonio de Alarcón** – *San Torcuato (on the Murcia road)* – ☎ *958 66 49 86* – *Fax 958 66 17 21* – *23 caves* – *€69* – 🍽 *€5.34*. The only drawback of these beautifully decorated, centrally heated caves is their proximity to the motorway, although this is compensated for by their almost perfect natural soundproofing. Facilities include a restaurant serving local dishes and a swimming pool.

In Loja

🍴🛏 **Finca La Bobadilla** – *18km/11mi W along the A 92; turn off at the Villanueva de Tapia exit* – ☎ *958 32 18 61* – *Fax 958 32 18 10* – 🖵 – *52 rooms, 10 suites* – *€235/320 (including breakfast)*. This luxury hotel is tucked away on an estate covering some 350ha/865 acres. The suites here have hosted heads of state, including King Juan Carlos, and leading international stars such as Plácido Domingo and Tom Cruise. The estate is a village in itself and even has its own church, the bells of which ring out every morning.

In Priego de Córdoba

🍴 **Villa Turística de Priego** – *In the village of Zagrilla, 7km/4.5mi from Priego* – ☎ *957 70 35 03* – *Fax 957 70 35 73* – 🖵 – *47 apartments, 5 rooms* – *€50.50/68.30* – 🍽 *€5.50*. The villa comprises a series of apartments for between one and four guests in a verdant setting of pomegranate trees, jasmine and a whole host of other flowers.

In The Sierra Nevada

🍴🛏 **Kenia Nevada** – *Virgen de las Nieves, 6* – ☎ *958 48 09 11* – *Fax 958 48 08 07* – *66 rooms, 1 suite* – *€78.70/140* – 🍽 *€12*. The hotel's harmonious style, characterised by a profusion of wood and stone, blends in perfectly with the delightful scenery around it. Pleasant indoor pool and warm, cosy bedrooms.

Bars and Cafés

A combination of two main factors – the large number of university students in Granada and the cold temperatures here in winter – is behind the city's extensive choice of bars, cafés and nightclubs. Calle Pedro Antonio de Alarcón (popular with university students) and the carrera del Darro, close to both the Alhambra and the Albaicín district, tend to be more popular with a younger crowd.

Bohemia Jazz Café – *Santa Teresa, 17 – Open 3pm-2am (3am Fri-Sat).* Popular with a cross-section of customers who come to this delightful café for a quiet drink and a chat with friends to a backdrop of jazz-inspired decoration and music. Of the four pianos here, three are true collectors' items, one of which is played several times a week by a resident pianist. Seven types of top-quality arabica coffee are available here.

El Tren – *Carril del Picón, 22 – Open 8am-10pm.* This unusual bar has a warm and friendly atmosphere and an extensive choice of teas, coffees and cakes. The bar has an electric train running on tracks suspended from the ceiling, hence the name. A varied clientele which changes according to the time of day.

Las Teterías – Calle Calderería Nueva, between the city centre and the Albaicín, is a good example of a street found in the Moorish quarter of any city. The small and cosy *teterías* are typical cafés which give a welcoming feel to this particular street. Two are worth mentioning: the quiet and pleasant **Pervane**, with its huge selection of teas, coffees, milk shakes and cakes; and **Kasbah**, decorated with cushions and rugs on the floor in true Moorish coffee shop style.

S. Ollivier/MICHELIN **Las Alpujarras**

La Fontana – *Carrera del Darro, 19 (next to the first bridge) – Open 4pm-3am*. Housed in an old residence at the foot of the Alhambra and Albaicín hills, this inviting antique-adorned café is an ideal place for a quiet drink in an atmosphere dominated by lively conversation. An excellent choice of coffees, herbal teas and cocktails.

El 3er Aviso – *Plaza de Toros, 1-18 – Open 4pm-5am*. A surprising location inside the city's bullring, where its spacious design combines with modern, tasteful decor. The café is located on several floors, and from each floor it is possible to look down onto the floors below. Good chart music popular with the 25-45 crowd, and also quiet areas for those wanting to enjoy a chat.

El Príncipe – *Campo del Príncipe, 7. Open in summer, Tue-Sun, 11pm-6am; in winter, Wed-Sat, 11pm-6am*. This large venue is the place to be seen for the city's in-crowd, hosting regular concerts by leading Spanish groups. Always crowded with a mix of ages.

El Camborio – *Sacromonte, 47 (on Sacromonte hill) – Open Tue-Sat, midnight to 6 or 7am*. One of Granada's oldest and most established nocturnal haunts which has been open for the past 30 years. Best approached by car or taxi as it is located in one of the city's least salubrious districts. The venue itself is quite unique with four inter-connected caves and good dance music. Popular with an eclectic crowd, though predominantly frequented by students.

*E*ntertainment

Granada's cultural traditions are still as strong as ever with a range of events on offer throughout the year. The Teatro Alhambra *(calle Molinos, 54 – ☎ 958 22 04 47)* hosts a varied season of theatre which is complemented by the programme of high-quality concerts at the Auditorio Manuel de Falla.

The city also organises a regular and varied range of shows and exhibitions, full details of which are listed in a monthly magazine on sale at newspaper stands around the city. Granada's City Hall also publishes a monthly guide with details of cultural events throughout the province. This guide is readily available from tourist offices.

Along The Costa Tropical

La Herradura has developed into an important centre for scuba diving. A number of dive companies operate here offering courses for all levels. These include Buceo La Herradura *(Puerto Deportivo de Marina del Este, ☎ 958 82 70 83)* and Granada Sub *(Paseo Andrés Segovia, 6, ☎ 958 64 02 81)*.

In Loja

For those visitors keen on fishing, the nearby village of Riofrío has its own fishing area, the Coto Intensivo de Pesca, which is open all year round. *For permits, information and reservations, contact the Albergue de Pescadores de Riofrío, ☎ 958 32 31 77 or 958 32 11 56.*

Shopping

Granada's principal shopping area is located along the main avenues in the city centre and in the adjoining pedestrianised streets. The heart of this area is Gran Vía de Colón, calle Reyes Católicos and calle Recogidas, with their mix of traditional shops, modern boutiques and the occasional shopping centre, such as the Neptuno in calle Recogidas.

The former Moorish silk market, the Alcaicería, is located in the same area, next to the cathedral. Nowadays, this maze of narrow alleyways is home to souvenir and craft shops in an area that still retains its Moorish atmosphere. Another typical sight in this part of the city is the plethora of flower stalls which add a delightful splash of colour to plaza de Bib-Rambla.

The typical crafts of Granada include inlaid wood, particularly on small objects such as small boxes and jewellery cases, and pottery. Examples of these items can be found in the Alcaicería.

The same area is also home to a number of pastry shops *(pastelerías)* selling the typical *piononos*, the traditional delicacy of Granada. Those on sale at the Pastelería Flor y Nata, in calle Reyes Católicos, are worthy of their long-established reputation.

Every Sunday a market selling wares of every description is held at the Campo de la Feria on the carretera de Jaén.

In the Alpujarras

Jarapas – The typical local rugs *(jarapas)* of the area can be found throughout the Alpujarras. Two workshops in Pampaneira are particularly recommended for their handmade products: Hilacar *(calle Viso – ☎ 956 76 32 26)* and La Rueca *(calle José Antonio, 4 – ☎ 958 76 30 27)*.

Cured hams – The best place to buy cured hams is Trevélez, where there are a number of drying sheds.

Imagen © TURISMO ANDALUZ S.A.   **Small market in the Albayzín district**

*I*ndex

Director	David Brabis
Series Editor	Ana González
Editorial team	Jeremy Kerrison, Alison Hughes
Picture Editor	Alexandra Rosina
Mapping	Michèle Cana, Daniel Duguay
Graphic Coordination	Marie-Pierre Renier, Marc Pinard
Graphics	Jean-Luc Cannet
Typesetting	Didier Hée
Production	Renaud Leblanc
Marketing	Ellie Danby
Sales	John Lewis (UK), Robin Bird (USA)

Manufacture Française des Pneumatiques MICHELIN
Société en commandite par actions au capital de 304 000 000 €
Place des Carmes-Déchaux - 63000 Clermont-Ferrand (France)
R.C.S. Clermont-Fd B 855 200 507

© Michelin et Cie, Propriétaires-éditeurs
Dépot légal mai 2005 - ISBN 2-06-711544-8
Printed in France 04-05/1.1

No part of this publication may be reproduced in any form
without the prior permission of the publisher.

Typesetting: NORD COMPO, Villeneuve-d'Ascq (France)
Printing-binding: POLLINA, Luçon (Francia) - L97201

MICHELIN TRAVEL PUBLICATIONS
Hannay House - 39 Clarendon Road - WATFORD, WD17 1JA
☎ 01923 205240 - Fax 01923 205241
www.ViaMichelin.com - TheGreenGuide-uk@uk.michelin.com